Theater of
Architecture

Theater of Architecture

Architecture

Hugh Hardy

Conversations
with Mildred Friedman

Princeton Architectural Press, New York

Hugh Hardy, 1960

Hardy Holzman Pfeiffer Associates, 1969

Preface

This book presents my thoughts about the practice of architecture through examples of twenty projects for which I was partner in charge. Except for the first, a residence that helps to define a New York City street, all have been designed for public use. They were selected to show diversity, contrasting a variety of functions and aesthetics as a way to move beyond questions of surface appearance. The physical, historical, and cultural context of each is different, and they receive the public in many different ways. Yet, as I review them now, they somehow seem more joined by a common sensibility than I first imagined. Even though these projects do not all look the same, they all were created with the intention of setting the stage for their inhabitants' different journeys of discovery.

I imagine this may be the result of my affection for theater. Such an affinity is suspect to most architects because of theater's basis in emotion, artifice, and surprising human behavior. But its dedication to emotional truth and a poetic interpretation of the physical world can be of great value to those who try to understand how the public responds to architecture.

My ambition for the pages that follow is to create a view of architecture that transcends categories of style or dictates of fashion. (These serve a useful but more limited purpose.) My intention is to discuss buildings in relation to what they do, how they do it, and how their context inevitably influences the results.

In theater, the complete context of a stage production—its setting and point of view—are as important as the original script. In architecture, a building—whether freestanding or deeply enmeshed in an urban grid—is equally influenced by its context. Just as in a play, public understanding, rather than some abstract, critical theory, is the ultimate measure of success. But remember: both public affection and critical values may change, ultimately leaving you the judge. Join me now in consideration of how context and continuity influence architectural design.

The following twenty projects were realized over forty years of architectural practice and include work from Hardy Holzman Pfeiffer Associates (HHPA) and H3 Hardy Collaboration Architecture (H3). Although conceived in collaboration with other people, these are the projects that represent most clearly my personal commitment to both the client and the design.

In addition to my own commentary, presented in ten chapters arranged by topic, I have also included an edited series of conversations between each client and Mildred Friedman, former editor of *Design Quarterly* at the Walker Art Center in Minneapolis. Her broad knowledge of contemporary architecture has been an invaluable resource. I am most grateful for her insight and skill. It was her idea that discussions about each project's origins could be a way to discover how its results match its original intent.

A word about H3: this firm, now eight years old, is the third that I have helped originate. The first was Hugh Hardy & Associates, a fledgling office originally staffed by myself and two others. In fact, there were no associates. It was sustained by freelance work and the good fortune of a major commission to design a residence in Ottawa, Canada. We were located in an old rooming house at 18 West Twenty-Fifth Street, with neighboring views of a true flophouse. It offered the kind of cheap accommodations no longer found near Madison Square. My future partners turned up by accident while they were searching for work, and without any specific plan, we took advantage of our different points of view to collaborate on a variety of design projects.

The exuberance of youth led us to challenge the status quo. To establish interesting, low-budget spatial volumes and to save money, we exposed the raw reality of buildings' structural, mechanical, and electrical systems. Visible framing, unpainted aluminum electrical conduits, and brightly painted air ducts, all enjoying an unbridled use of color, characterized our work.

Establishment of Hardy Holzman Pfeiffer Associates came naturally, as the three of us challenged each other yet found common agreement about the nature of architectural design. When we formed our partnership in the late 1960s, we were young upstarts, barely professional. Until the firm grew to almost fifty people, we still had no associates. As it expanded, we included many different talents filling different roles. We ultimately became bicoastal, with offices in Los Angeles and New York and a total population of more than one hundred.

Before disbanding this remarkable practice with its distinguished list of accomplishments, we won ten American Institute of Architects (AIA) National Design Awards and received considerable professional and public attention. We

were registered by the State of New York as being led by a collaborative group rather than an individual, as most firms were at that time. When the American Academy of Arts and Letters awarded us its Arnold W. Brunner Memorial Prize in 1974, all three partners were named. We were the first to be so honored.

Under the pressure of business, the founding partners grew apart. When our personal three-way exchanges grew to be less about design and more about administration, the time came to go our separate ways. It had become obvious that we had already established three different operations under the HHPA umbrella, and in 2004 we formally disbanded, although we all continue to individually operate practices that emphasize collaboration. It was simple for Norman Pfeiffer to maintain his office in Los Angeles (since expanded to New York), renamed Pfeiffer Partners, while Malcolm Holzman established his own organization across town in Manhattan as Holzman Moss Bottino, and I retained half of the floor space of the original New York HHPA.

This time I have a staff of thirty, and we call ourselves H3 Hardy Collaboration Architecture. After six years of successful practice, H3 announced its future lies with five new partners: Ariel Fausto, John Fontillas, Geoff Lynch, Jack Martin, and Daria Pizzetta—no doubt the subject of a future volume. My new partners are the latest in an ever-growing list of collaborators that gives me great professional pride.

H3 Hardy Collaboration Architecture, 2012

Contrast: Lower Manhattan, 2012

Introduction

I have been a practicing architect for more than half my adult life—a vocation that has produced results that have been encouraging and discouraging but never dull. In the process, despite wide changes in society, technology, and my profession, my approach to work has continuously advanced without a preconceived agenda or any doctrinaire assumptions about what architecture should be, other than a logical and enjoyable response to questions of shelter. Instead, I have been guided by my honest explorations of the specific needs of each project rather than the adherence to any dogma or style. I therefore prefer my work to remain unclassified, with each project considered individually.

Everything in our consumer society can be bought or sold as a disposable commodity—whether goods, politicians, or high-style buildings. To reach marketplace dominance, each seller competes to establish a clearly identified "brand." However, I do not believe the true purpose of architecture lies in promotion of commercial identity through buildings intended to establish a brand, either for client or architect. Instead, the profession's true strength lies in the building of communities. Rather than concentrating on brand development, I propose architects should serve the common interests of those communities by enhancing their experiences. It is clear that a working knowledge of theater has been a great asset to me in this approach to making architecture.

Some maintain that once again a new era of design has arrived, ushered in by the form-giving made possible by the technological revolution. They believe that the present is unfettered by the rhetoric of the past. But before we proclaim the future and craft the requisite new manifesto, remember: no truly successful transformation in the spirit of architecture can occur without recognition of what has gone before. Architecture continues to be a language, one whose continuity is crucial. New ideas, techniques, and technologies must be embraced while acknowledging that each generation inevitably establishes its own set of values within the framework of history. Future architectural results may be different and their physical scale and audacity of accomplishment perhaps even greater, but the essential challenge remains the same: to find ways to connect people in a community. This requires a thorough understanding of how humanity's only constant—its quixotic nature—can be enhanced by a new architecture.

Writing about architecture is only a surrogate for true involvement. Architecture must be understood through direct experience, by moving around and through it. Pictures may help or distort, and theory may inform or confuse; only experience reveals the actual intent and accomplishments of building, which represents a language to record human ambition. Given an awareness of their context and use, together with an understanding of the design intent that brought them into being, buildings of a particular era can offer rewarding cultural insight about earlier times. Architecture, while it embraces the past, can also help anticipate the future. Because it exists in both past and present, it can become part of a continuum of promise, in which the built environment is a record of many different points of view. However, its creators must always live in the future tense.

Diversity is an inherent part of life. For instance, Darwin's theory of evolution is based upon the discovery that the random cross-pollination of flowers is accomplished by insects. Without this process, plants would be able only to self-fertilize for generation after generation, producing unvarying clones (rather like mindlessly repeated institutional architecture). Biological diversity permits plants to adapt to changing climate, just as architectural diversity enriches a society's ability to respond to changing needs.

The physical, social, geographic, financial, and historic context of each of our projects is as important to their design as the activities they house. Any new construction is conceived in the theoretical world but is located within the physical fact of each community. Just as the total activity of theatergoing involves an experience far greater than the performance itself, the experience of architecture includes much more than what happens when one either sees a building at a distance or enters its front door. Although architecture is thought of as fixed and permanent, it is in constant transition all around us, and the past is easily forgotten as new replaces old. Even without outright demolition, buildings can be completely altered in appearance and meaning through construction of new neighboring structures that offer a new physical context, sometimes with humorous results.

In New York City, you would expect to find architecture a topic of constant public discussion. But until 9/11, few outside the profession discussed it, and most new work was dismissed out of hand as unworthy and conventional, inferior to that found in other cities with more cutting-edge design cultures. In fact, the spirit of many of New York's great monuments did originate in places far from Manhattan. The Seagram Building and the original Museum of Modern Art, not to mention the United Nations complex, reflect brave ideas of European modernism that are all more fully realized elsewhere. But since 9/11's horrors, the subsequent agony of planning for rebuilding a major part of the city has become a collective responsibility that has encouraged people to talk openly about architectural

design and freely express opinions that were once the province of professionals.

When I attended architecture school in the 1950s, history was thought to be a trap for the unmindful. At best it was regarded as misplaced sentiment, at worst, as aesthetic corruption. It was said that a new age demanded an architecture that was also new, totally abstract, and without reference to the past.

Nor was the use of color part of the standard curriculum. Modernist architecture did not require it, and color reproduction was not widely found in magazines or books. Kodachrome slides and Kodak Carousel projectors were not yet omnipresent. The digital world did not exist. Design was dominated by modernism's prescription of rectangular plans in black and white, organized by structural grids grouping like activities in separate areas all connected by straight, straight corridors. It appeared to be a simple formula, often based upon the spare and repetitive design of factories flooded with natural light— easy to create (if boring to experience), often showing little hint of originality.

I am part of a generation that rejected these modernist orthodoxies. We students inherited its original promise of an idealized new social order that would be realized through architecture. But by the 1950s, that vision had become stale. Almost all of us found it boring and challenged the status quo with a search for less-rigid theories and a variety of new forms. My early work with HHPA explored layered architectural plans, an aggressive use of color, and the exposure of the functional systems that inhabit architecture. Others reacted by inventing radical new shapes or reinventing past historical forms, adding a layer of irony. Still others developed open-plan designs that supported an informal and flexible approach to organizing activities, or introduced sensuous curves or unorthodox, vertical vistas into modernism's horizontals. A few inventively pursued the use of new materials and technologies in the name of progress and environmental responsibility.

Contemporary design theory is no longer cut off from tradition, even as critical judgment has become increasingly difficult due to astonishing changes in program intent, systems of form-giving and spatial organization, and technology. We live in a period of great aesthetic richness, but it is accompanied by much confusion. The built landscape of America testifies to a startling range of aesthetic and economic concerns, as embodied by its high-rise mixed-use buildings, commercial strips, air-conditioned malls, suburban housing developments, reused or restored older buildings, and a multitude of other expressions. Juxtapositions of great vulgarity and variety continue to be the order of the American landscape. Taken as a whole, this physical exuberance overwhelms the theoretical, as a constantly changing public realm responds to latest market trends in an apparently endless search for profit.

The profit motive can debase or enhance results; many of New York's finest buildings were built to make money. These have not, however, been the product of formula. Architecture need not be pedestrian in order to be profitable; with imagination, even meager resources can bring delight.

Henry Ford is often quoted as having said, "History is bunk," but even his pursuit of the new has become a part of America's historical context and still shapes contemporary ideas about industrial production. The passage of time changes everything, causing the new to become old, along with those who create it. A building's public understanding and appreciation change, even as its appearance remains unaltered. The illusion that restoration can somehow prevent the advance of time leads to sentimental re-creations of candied sweetness—places of make-believe.

It is possible to incorporate an awareness of the past into contemporary designs without copying specific forms. A new design can exhibit a sensitivity to context and history, or it can stand in isolation. But the strongest work comes from recognition that the language of architecture can speak authoritatively across generations.

Top Seagram Building,
New York, New York, 1958

Middle Museum of Modern Art,
New York, New York, 1939

Bottom United Nations Headquarters,
New York, New York, 1952

In our society of volatility and change, efforts to preserve the past have sometimes caused radical confrontations between those who believe in the inherent value of the new and those who prefer to keep their memories. No one would now like to live the way even the wealthiest nineteenth-century New Yorkers once did, despite the imagined glamour of horse-drawn carriages and deferential servants. Life without the conveniences of indoor plumbing, electricity, air conditioning, home appliances, electronic communication, or automobiles would now be unacceptable. Nonetheless, the authority and grandeur of earlier architecture still has great appeal, and it is instructive for us to see and experience buildings that earlier generations valued, even as we use them so differently.

When my architectural practice began, the preservation movement was still nascent. America had always been the land of the new, a place of constant improvement where technological advance was taken for granted. But the 1963 destruction of Penn Station, that heroic but unwieldy monument, soured this myth. As streets became filled with banal contemporary construction, new could no longer be assumed to be better. Penn Station's destruction was the catalyst for a change in attitude, leading directly to the formation of the New York City Landmarks Preservation Commission in 1965. Some viewed this as an opportunity to freeze the city in time. But landmarks law contains recognition of change and permits it if the commission finds a change appropriate. Ultimately, saving the built environment is for the benefit of future generations; the past can educate people in ways that isolation of architectural dogma cannot.

Replication is not the goal of restoration. Although techniques of reproduction and simulation are ever-advancing, surrogates for real material qualities can offer only the illusion of authenticity. In her 1997 book *The Unreal America*, Ada Louise Huxtable discussed the label "authentic reproduction," used by the Colonial Williamsburg Foundation to denote products for sale in their gift shops:

General Motors Technical Center, Warren, Michigan, Eero Saarinen, 1956

Top Whitaker Center, Harrisburg, Pennsylvania, HHPA, 1999

Middle Ray and Maria Stata Center at MIT, Cambridge, Massachusetts, Frank Gehry, 2004

Bottom CityCenter, Las Vegas, Nevada, Ehrenkrantz, Eckstut & Kuhn Architects, 2004

I cannot think of a more mischievous, dangerous, anomalous, and shoddy perversion of language and meaning. A perfect contradiction in terms, it makes no sense at all; but what particularly offends is its smug falseness, its dissembling, genteel pretentiousness. . . . To equate a replica with the genuine artifact is the height of sophistry; it cheapens and renders meaningless its true age and provenance. . . . What is missing is the original mind, hand, material, and eye. The kindest thing you can say is that an authentic reproduction is a genuine oxymoron.

Huxtable identifies Williamsburg as where the public began a journey of misinformation about our relationship to the past.

New York is traditionally known as a place of the new, but its street plan bears unparalleled witness to the aims and life of earlier generations, providing an authentic sense of place. These streets perhaps constitute the city's ultimate landmark. As physical uniformity increases across America, cities become a more and more valuable source of authenticity; their dialogue between old and new is essential to contemporary culture and cannot be simulated in vacuum-molded plastic. The immediate cultural discoveries found in landmark structures help define both the past and present city, giving each generation responsibility for passing on their record of ambition and achievement to those who follow. But how is this best done?

We now have many high-tech ways for studying and attempting to revisit the past, from online archives of historical documents to methods of paint analysis and material replication. However, it is impossible to fully re-create the experience of living in any era of the past. Although traditional construction materials and techniques still exist, contemporary perceptions have greatly changed from those of previous generations. Our forbears lived in a different visual culture, making their perception of design far different from our own. We have been exposed to

the vast amplification of contemporary architecture's large scale and its new materials palette. Awareness of enclosure has become much different, now making places seem small that once seemed large. But even more subtly, our sensibilities have changed in ways that make earlier forms, colors, textures, and surfaces appear foreign, not commonplace. For all the contemporary scientific dedication to the past, we can only interpret what went before, providing at best a simulation adjusted to contemporary sensibilities.

Preservation no longer needs to be justified. In fact, it was public pressure that pushed the architectural profession to accept the idea that restoration is of benefit. Originally not thought to be worthy of attention by important designers, the reuse of historic structures now receives almost as much critical attention as the building of new ones. But rediscovering the past can be tricky. The goal of turning the clock back raises questions about which era of a building's life was the most authentic. Although favored by historians, reconstruction of a building's earliest appearance is typically the most conjectural, and subsequent alterations may have included valuable design ideas.

All this quickly leads to the conclusion that total restoration is basically impossible and most likely illegal. Not only have we, the public, changed in our aesthetic sensibility and our demands for safety and personal comfort, the materials and skills required for building and the surrounding cultural associations have drastically changed as well. Most startling of all, our buildings are currently illuminated with two to three times as much light as those of past centuries, and the color of artificial light even now is rapidly changing. Gone is the flickering orange-yellow glow of gaslight and the comforting warmth of incandescent light bulbs. These are becoming illegal due to their inefficient use of energy, and are already being succeeded by the building-code-mandated bluish glare of LED light sources. Even more difficult to accommodate, building-code requirements for life safety and wheelchair access require an increase in dimensions that puts current law at odds

---

*Ada Louise Huxtable, *The Unreal America: Architecture and Illusion* (New York: New Press, 1997), 18.

Left Pennsylvania Station, New York, New York, demolition, 1963
Right The Packer Collegiate Institute, Brooklyn, New York, HHPA, 2003

with history, confirming that (as in Thomas Wolfe's great novel) "you can't go home again."

However, the ease and speed with which buildings are now conceived and built, whatever their aesthetic premise, produces a temptation to attempt simulation instead of pursuing authenticity. In fact, some architecture is becoming akin to scenery in its limited lifespan and preoccupation with decorative surface appeal. As a result, theater has again begun to influence architecture.

An early influence of theater on my thinking about architectural design was my time working as an assistant to Jo Mielziner, then the most distinguished scene designer on Broadway. I was one of his draftsmen, given such tasks as drawing elevations for various sets of the 1959 musical *Gypsy*. Mielziner was the most poetic design professional in American theater. His unequaled gifts led to the realization of scenery, costume, and lighting designs that represented a unique level of artistic achievement. He transformed the meager spaces of Broadway theaters into realms of magical experience. All this was made possible by his unrivaled ability to invent productions whose emotional resonance stemmed from the power of abstracted imagery that distilled the dramatic essence of onstage storytelling.

By "theater" I suggest more than the surprise of make-believe—I mean life-enhancing experience that reveals human nature in all of its variety. Collaboration forms the constant

substance of working in theater. In performance, the work of stagehands is as important as what stars do. Playwrights and directors must work together, and designers must balance their concepts with directors' needs. This interdependency has taught me to value the discoveries found in a collaborative setting and has shaped my inclusive approach to work in the public realm.

When Mielziner and Eero Saarinen were commissioned to collaborate on the design of Lincoln Center's Vivian Beaumont Theater, I became directly involved as a liaison between the two. Because I had degrees in architecture and was also a member of the United Scenic Artists, local USA 829 (having once believed that my future lay in scenic design), I was able to both draw scenery and represent Mielziner in meetings with Saarinen about the new theater. Although they had known each other from World War II, when they had worked together in the US Army's camouflage unit, their minds operated in completely different ways. Mielziner did things by instinct. He felt rather than thought about what was appropriate to the mood and structure of each theatrical production, drawing on a powerful artistic vision. Saarinen analyzed his way through the design process, treating it as a highly thoughtful investigation. He viewed design as problem solving, part of an inevitable advance toward a better future. It was my job to translate the ideas of each into language the other would understand.

Left Mahaiwe Theater, Great Barrington, Massachusetts, Joseph McArthur Vance, 1905
Right Mahaiwe Theater, restoration by H3 Hardy Collaboration Architecture, 2006

Mielziner's design for the 1949 production of Arthur Miller's *Death of a Salesman*, revived on Broadway in 2012, clearly was an integral part of this landmark work's emotional power. It gave a brooding power to the salesman's skeletal house, sometimes enclosed by an encroaching prison of brick tenements and sometimes transformed by the use of projected springtime leaves to re-create the same neighborhood as a sunny, green place of memory. The combination of these scenic elements in a fluid sequence borrowed from cinema was new to Broadway. Both Miller and Elia Kazan, the play's original director, worked to achieve the lyrical flow of action that was the hallmark of this production.

Writing in the *New York Times* of March 15, 2012, Ben Brantley notes that Mielziner's production of more than sixty years ago was a "beautiful, lyrical ghostly vision—appropriate to a play in which an idealized past haunts an unforgiving present." Mielziner's theatrical interpretations explored an entire gamut of scenic configurations. He combined solid and transparent forms with great washes of painted backgrounds, illuminated on both sides, whose composition could be altered through changes in lighting. In fact, his command of stage light inaugurated a new era for the manipulation of the narrow dimensions of Broadway's obsolete stages. His was never a literal transcription of time and place but always a heightened representation of both, creating places that were more real for existing onstage, their lasting power enhanced by memory.

Saarinen had grown up with architecture, playing under his father's drafting table in Finland. Drawing and design were always part of his life, perhaps to a point of obsession. Little else held equal importance, and by the 1950s, when he established his own office in Bloomfield Hills, Michigan, he was a major force in America, whether in planning, building and furniture design, or industrial design.

Far from a formulaic approach to design, Saarinen's method was intellectual exploration, an ordering process that resulted in highly original forms. He responded to neither dogma nor preconceived ideas. The results of his method were unlike anything I had previously encountered. Although a confirmed modernist, Saarinen designed no two buildings that looked the same, upsetting conventional professional wisdom and prevailing theories of unified form giving. His curiosity was relentless, and he constantly explored why our surroundings had to be formed in conventional ways. He challenged relationships among floors, ceiling, and walls; the bond between structure and architectural form; and the conflicting movements of people and cars. No detail was too small to escape his attention, and always there was the challenge: "Why do it this way?" In his high-energy office environment, filled with enormously talented people, giant models, and this intense spirit of inquiry, I discovered for the first time the glories of creating a truly contemporary architecture.

Saarinen believed the Beaumont represented an opportunity to build something new. Lincoln Center had asked for a repertory theater in which to perform contemporary productions of classical plays, much as other Lincoln Center companies presented the classics of opera, ballet, or symphony orchestra. New works would also be staged, but this was not to be a commercial Broadway theater, and Saarinen took the program as a mandate for using the new form of the thrust stage (one that extends performance into the theater auditorium with seating on three sides). Believing the proscenium format obsolete and the thrust stage the form of the future, Saarinen saw it as part of an inevitable progression (like the evolution from train to car to airplane) and insisted on using it for the Beaumont. This form was greatly disliked by Mielziner, who had spent his distinguished career working in proscenium theaters and thought thrust stages a fad.

Saarinen initially had proposed they divide up their responsibilities. He would design the auditorium, and Mielziner would be responsible for everything backstage, behind wherever the curtain line would be drawn. Instead they battled it out to an enforced compromise: a flexible scheme was adopted in which the auditorium could accommodate modified forms of both proscenium and thrust stages. Difficult to use and at first regarded a failure, the result has proved itself over time as a theater found nowhere else, a stimulating environment where magical productions regularly take place.

I now realize how much I was influenced by Saarinen. My exposure to this astonishingly driven and insightful individual convinced me that architecture, not theater, would be my future. Although his early death at age fifty-one precluded my intention to leave New York and work directly with him in his newly established Connecticut office, it is now clear how much I responded to Saarinen's dedication to problem solving and how it continued to be a powerful influence on my emerging sensibilities.

Explorations of twenty projects follow, presented in ten categories and grouped for contrast or to reinforce common values. Taken all together they are testament to my belief in diversity and to the influence of theater in my work.

For example, the obvious contrast between the Harvey Theater at the Brooklyn Academy of Music and Radio City Music Hall, both in New York City, can reveal how each theater's configuration appeals to a different community and is useful for a different type of stage presentation. Both are restorations. Both investigate the past. But the experience of each is different because of its individual design premise. One is not better than the other; both can generate extraordinary experiences.

A number of projects consider restoration and its complex manipulation of time. If the results are to be fully authentic, a desire to turn the clock back has to be knowledgeably accommodated. Although several such projects are included, none is an exact reproduction. The past is honored not through scrupulous accuracy but rather with a balance between original intent and contemporary need. The results may be impure, but I maintain that they are more honest in their affectionate displays than any effort to make an old building look brand new. Such an approach robs a building of its own history, and although many such examples continue to win awards and delight the public with their gilded charms, this method of bringing a building back to imagined life is like putting lipstick on a corpse.

Another aim of this book's organization is to emphasize the importance of context. Projects in Cooperstown, New York, are designed to directly respond to that remarkable lakeside community as well as fulfill their program uses. The federal courthouse in Jackson, Mississippi, is greatly influenced by its position on axis with the State Capitol, while the café in New York City's Bryant Park responds to its park setting, and the shopping development Ridge Hill in Yonkers invents its own contemporary setting reminiscent of a small

Westchester town. Context thus becomes an essential contributor to architectural form.

Other sections explore such topics as entry, a basic element of the experience of any building. The New York Botanical Garden's visitor's center establishes landscape as a basic element of visitors' experiences, while the Rainbow Bridge Port of Entry at Niagara Falls prepares visitors from Canada and those leaving the United States for international discovery, with the dramatic backdrop of this world-famous site. A section on public space considers the differences among public projects—those generated by developers and those created by public-private partnership. Concerns for the environment and a responsible use of energy are addressed in a discussion of the natural ventilation at the Opera Theater of the Glimmerglass Festival in Cooperstown, New York, while the sophisticated design of mechanical systems and an architectural use of plants at the Botanical Research Institute of Texas in Fort Worth represent the latest technological methods.

Finally, the three new theaters discussed in the book's last section, although different in their architecture, have a common goal of providing an intimate setting for the exploration of new work. With subsidized ticket prices and seating capacities smaller than off-Broadway minimums, they also represent a way to attract new, younger audiences. These are nonprofit production houses dedicated to ideas, not box-office revenue, and represent a change from thinking about theater as commerce.

There are many ways to make truly contemporary architecture outside of the constraints of formula or dogma. Each generation has the responsibility to pass the built environment on to the next without the damage or wholesale destruction caused by utopian theories. Change is inevitable, but, as these projects show, there is no single measure of importance, whether a building be old or new. Let us keep a balance in our environment, in order to build a livable, appealing, and diverse twenty-first century for those who follow.

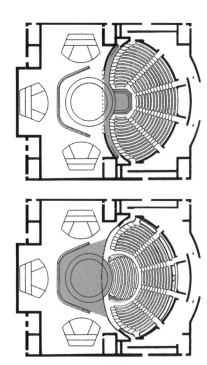

Top Thrust stage plan for Vivian Beaumont Theater, Lincoln Center, New York, New York, Eero Saarinen

Middle Beaumont Theater interior, Eero Saarinen, completed in 1965

Bottom Sketch for Arthur Miller's *Death of a Salesman*, Jo Mielziner, 1949

A Talisman

"This project—mixing old and new and accepting the changes brought by time when working with building preservation— has served as a talisman for many of my designs."

18 West Eleventh Street
New York, New York

Conversation
Kent Barwick
Former president of the
Municipal Art Society of
New York and former chair of
the New York City Landmarks
Preservation Commission

I use the word "talisman" to describe this prophetic early work—a single project whose ideas have been echoed throughout my career. In the case of 18 West Eleventh Street, this building brought great public attention to my design ideas and made visible my emerging interest in "impure" design.

Project

18 West Eleventh Street
New York, New York, 1979

It was built to replace a townhouse in Greenwich Village that had been accidentally destroyed by bombs being manufactured by young dissidents in its cellar. This was the first design of a new building presented to the New York City Landmarks Preservation Commission under its first full-time chairman, Harmon Goldstone. Despite the opinions of some of his commissioners, Goldstone did not believe a reproduction of the original house was appropriate.

In the March 10, 1971, *New York Times*, Ada Louise Huxtable wrote:

Mr. Hardy was not willing to pretend that there was no bomb. Or that history of another kind is not now part of West Eleventh Street. Architecture is not a stage set: it is the continuing evidence of a city's reality. Nothing can bring number 18 to life again. The house is dead; long live the house.

I had proposed a design that is part reproduction and part invention, using brick and architectural details that matched the original facade but also including casement windows and an angled form inserted in the middle of the facade—a response intended to express the interior's diagonal plan.

Preservationists wanted the original building reproduced. I could not deny the earlier existence of the site's five originally identical facades, but at the same time there existed no accurate record of their original design, so any reconstruction could be based solely on simulation and conjecture. Meanwhile, modernists would have preferred a dramatic contrast in glass and steel, breaking apart the row's original continuity. My solution was an impure combination and therefore offensive to both extremes, although its expression of the architectural problem is clearly stated.

This project—an example of mixing old and new and accepting the changes brought by time when working with building preservation—has served as a talisman for many of my subsequent designs. Its involvement with the relationship of old to new in the public life of the street foreshadows the direction of much of my work, whether on Main Street in Cooperstown, New York, or Court Street in Jackson, Mississippi.

18 West Eleventh Street
New York, New York

Number Eighteen West Eleventh Street was one
of five dwellings constructed as a speculative
real-estate development by Henry Brevoort in the
1840s. Over time, these initially identical facades
underwent various additions and improvements
in response to changing needs and fashions.

This street was once a very peaceful, even sleepy,
part of the city, but, astonishingly, one morning on
March 6, 1970, 18 West Eleventh Street erupted in
smoke and flames and was completely destroyed.
The owner's daughter, Cathy Wilkerson, had become
part of the radical political group the Weathermen,
and she had invited four young malcontents to join
her in the cellar of her Greenwich Village home
to make bombs. Their target was the library at
Columbia University; however, instead of creating a
new social order, they accidentally blew themselves
up. Wilkerson, along with one other member, Kathy
Boudin, escaped naked into the streets of New
York while the house was reduced to rubble.

My wife, Tiziana, upon reading about the blast in
the *New York Times* the following Sunday morning,
said, "We should buy the site and build a house
with the Masons." Patricia Mason was a successful
real-estate agent, particularly knowledgeable
about the Village, and her husband, Francis, was
an assistant to Arthur A. Houghton, president of
Steuben Glass. They had two children. We had two
children. They could have the bottom two floors with
a garden that would accommodate Pat's great love
of horticulture; we could have the top two floors
and create a sunny roof deck. I called the Masons
to propose the idea, and we soon jointly owned the
property. I began planning a two-family house.

The chairman of the Landmarks Commission, Harmon
Goldstone, asked me to propose a contemporary
design. He believed this was an excellent opportunity
to force the commission to consider the implications
of a contemporary scheme and avoid the easy
route of replication. For traditionalists, the chance
to place new architecture at such an infamous site
would require a faithful reconstruction of the original
structure. But none of the neighboring facades were

Kent Barwick
Former president of the
Municipal Art Society of New
York and former chair of the
New York City Landmarks
Preservation Commission

KB: I was at 18 West Eleventh
Street the night of the explosion.
I was living at 17 East Ninth
Street and went over and
watched it all. Later it came out
that the Weathermen had been
there. I was fascinated by the
explosion, as everybody was
in this bucolic neighborhood.

It was a revolutionary moment.
Kathy Boudin, who was Leonard
Boudin's daughter, was involved.
They were not people who were
flown in from Bulgaria with
bombs; they were kids who were
down from Vassar with bombs.

There came to be a public
discussion, prompted by Hugh's
plans, about how one would
respond to this missing tooth in
the facade of that south side of
Eleventh Street. The building that
was destroyed was not a unique
building; it was part of a row of
identical and not very distinguished
buildings. And so the missing-
tooth argument was that if
somebody punches you and you
lose your front tooth, do you put
it in white, or do you put it in with
stripes? And there was a very
strong argument that the right
thing to do was to put it back
exactly the same. And, of course,
the other argument is: You've got
to be kidding. This major thing

Left 18 West Eleventh Street,
prior to explosion, circa 1970

Right Construction begins in 1977

in their newborn condition. Changes in fenestration, decoration, handrails, and front door openings, as well as rooftop additions, had all been made.

No original documentation for the row existed, and any attempt to reproduce the original would obviously stand out from its neighbors. For instance, the front stairs of Number Twenty-Two had been removed for a street-level entry, and its brick facade was clad with white stucco. Therefore, if turning back the clock were truly necessary, would restoration be required for the whole row? Would it include removing the decorative Georgian panels added to Number Sixteen? Which of the two different existing handrails should be used, and which entrance door?

On the other hand, even in a city whose unending diversity of character, scale, and use defy consistency, the idea of a pure modernist design on this site seemed more disruptive to the row's appearance than complementary. Instead, this building exhibits traces of both a restoration and contemporary design processes in the form of a new central element that sets the front door and three bay windows in an angled recess. This composition announces the angled floor plan within and clearly marks the house as a contemporary insertion into the nineteenth-century row. Despite the new design's careful matching of the neighboring structures' brick and mortar, continuous cornice, upper-story windows, and original stoops, preservationists castigated the results as impure. Modernists, of course, denounced the whole thing as muddled and old-fashioned.

In 1971 the New York City Landmarks Preservation Commission approved the design by a vote of

happened in the history of the city of New York, and you just want to put it back as if it were an accidentally lost tooth? You can't do that, either.

I don't know who lives there now, but I do know that at the end of this high-minded discussion about American history and the place of the architect and the role of the dominant themes—at the end of this, whoever did occupy it had an affection for teddy bears. So ask any kid in the West Village, and they don't think of the Weathermen. All they think of is Paddington Bear.

This came along at a moment when there was kind of a growing backlash against the Landmarks Commission's attitude toward historic districts. The architects involved in the historic preservation movement in the 1960s were trained modernists. They were living in a world where it was imagined that cities could be very dramatically transformed.

Historic districts were sort of thrust into the political process in New York by people in Brooklyn Heights, because when the landmarks law was passed in 1965, they wanted their neighborhood protected. And they argued, I think rightly, that historic districts were well-established legally in the United States, in Charleston and

six to five. Commissioner William Conklin, architect of a respected apartment complex at 37 West Twelfth Street, complimented the design, citing its angled walls as being expressive of the force of the blast that destroyed the house. Alas, this poetic concept gave me too much credit, since my design was merely the result of traditional architectural thinking about relating outside and inside. At most, I wanted passersby to speculate about how a diagonal plan might animate the interior.

But we could not build. Mortgage rates and the cost of construction had escalated and our limited resources were insufficient, so, reluctantly, we placed the land on the market. For more than two years we found no interested buyer. Then the Langworthys appeared. Norma and David lived on Philadelphia's Main Line and were an adventuresome couple with grown children. They often sat at home at a bar that David had designed off their living room, enjoying the ritual of evening martinis in front of an enormous fish tank. Behind this, visible through a variety of swimming species, hung a big, pink neon sign proclaiming: "Norma's Bar." One night as they had their drinks together (straight up), knowing that all their friends were buying property in the Caribbean Islands, David asked Norma which island they should retire to. Without a pause, she said, "How about Manhattan?"

David and Norma had met at Carnegie Tech before it became Carnegie Mellon University, she studying acting, he scene design. David subsequently had worked for Donald Oenslager, a distinguished Broadway scenic designer, and they shared a lifelong devotion to theater. Their daughter had seen the "for sale" sign on the property and suggested the idea to her mother; the rest followed quickly. When they purchased the Eleventh Street property together with my landmark-approved design for the house, it seemed appropriate that I had worked for Jo Mielziner (Oenslager's professional rival) and was also enamored of theater. This created a special bond among the three of us.

The Langworthys' son Keith, a financial advisor, wanted to make certain the Landmarks Commission's Certificate of Appropriateness was still valid after so many years. He asked the commission. No one knew; the question had never come up before. The chair, Beverly Moss Spatt, ruled that the design must therefore be presented again before the current commissioners at a public hearing. When I made my

other places. And what was being tried in New York was something very, very different—an unusual approach, where you go in and pick one building—a public library or something—and say that it's a landmark, and the surrounding neighborhood isn't affected by it.

By the time the building was blown up, there were beginning to be people in the landmark-preservation movement for historic districts (again, led by Greenwich Village and Brooklyn Heights) who felt that the Landmarks Commission was being too permissive in what it was allowing to happen in historic districts. That was the atmosphere that Hugh came into with this project, that people were already beginning to say that the Landmarks Commission wasn't using the right standards.

The Village has always been one of the big battlegrounds in New York, because it's got a very verbal population of professional people who have access to the media, and there are a lot of lawyers who are prominent on Wall Street, and so therefore they know their way around. So the Village was always a contentious place. And in that sense, a good place—a crucible for ideas like this to be worked out.

second appearance before the commission, she did not allow me to either explain the origin of the design or acknowledge its previous approval. She announced that the history of the project would have no relevance to this presentation—I would only be permitted to review its aesthetic premise. However, we gained a second approval in 1977 (this time without poetic comments from any of the commissioners).

The house as built is similar to my original two-family design, although adjusted for a single family. A dramatic open stairwell was inserted from the basement to the roof. We designed a five-story diagonal plan to create longer spaces within the relatively narrow confines of the twenty-five-by-one-hundred-foot lot. The rear half of each floor sits a half-level above or below the front portion, and most areas are open to the central stairwell (with the exception of the master bedroom); this device creates unexpected views forming a rich catalogue of discovery as one moves through the various half-levels. I had originally intended that this geometry would lead to a diagonal entrance stair that would reinforce what lay inside. However, the Landmarks Commission found this too disturbing an interruption to the rhythm of repeating right angles made by existing stoops. We were asked instead to replicate the original staircase in precast stone.

This house continues to stand in concert with its neighbors, not quite the same as them but still linked to all of them by materials and decorative detail. The interior is a spatial surprise and a testament to the Langworthys' spirit of adventure. With the passage of time, continuity of the row has increased, as brick and mortar have aged and weathered, continuing to soften its appearance. Eighteen West Eleventh Street has become both a part of contemporary urban life and a provocative contribution to its history.

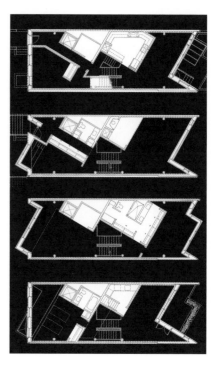

Floor plans

Entry

"Everyone knows the odd
feeling of joining a room full
of strangers. That moment
of entry is special, offering
delight, embarrassment,
or boredom. Buildings,
no less than people, can
make you feel welcome
or extraneous."

**New York Botanical Garden
Bronx, New York**

Conversation
Gregory Long
President of the New York
Botanical Garden

**Rainbow Bridge Port of Entry
Niagara Falls, New York**

Conversation
Allen Gandell
Former general manager
and CEO of the Niagara
Falls Bridge Commission

**United States
Federal Courthouse
Jackson, Mississippi**

Conversation
Judge William H. Barbour, Jr.
Senior judge for the Southern
District of Mississippi

"Entry" considers the experience of first viewing and then entering three different projects: a private institution, an international gateway, and a federal facility. Although each welcomes the public, the results differ widely.

Projects

New York Botanical Garden
Bronx, New York, 2004

Rainbow Bridge Port of Entry,
Niagara Falls, New York, 1998

United States Federal Courthouse
Jackson, Mississippi, 2010

Everyone knows the odd feeling of joining a room full of strangers. That moment of entry is special, offering delight, embarrassment, or boredom.

Buildings, no less than people, can make you feel welcome or extraneous. The front door was once the obvious focus of architectural entry; it had always been placed in the middle of a symmetrical facade. Modernists could not bear such hierarchical composition, with its traditional associations with royalty and decorative embellishments. They preferred freewheeling, spatially diverse schemes that assigned equal importance to each design element. The results were often asymmetrical compositions defined by isometric drawings rather than by the formality and fixed vantage point of one-point perspectives or rendered elevations. Instead of being conceived at eye level, these designs were made of abstract geometric forms isolated in space. These white volumes suspended in structural grids were arresting, but all this spatial drama obscured where to enter. Unless a site's landscape design featured a large plaza surrounding a visible entry, one often wondered: Where was the front door? Automobiles further complicated this dilemma by separating entry into separate channels—one for pedestrians, one for cars. There is little welcoming ceremony in the experience of walking through a parking garage in search of pedestrian access.

The experience of entering a building is more complex than quick recognition of its facade or the design of its doorway. It may involve the route of approach or the passage through a vestibule or some other enclosure. These elements must be clearly related and their experience must be carefully planned.

An entrance can be formal or informal, ambiguous or clearly focused, but its effects need to be considered as a basic part of architectural design.

Now that energy-saving vestibules or revolving doors are required to meet new building codes, I find it amusing that contemporary architecture has come full circle. This offers architects a new design challenge, since the vestibule denies modernism's dictate that outside and inside should be conceived as a seamless whole. The requirements of the current building code instead result in architecturally stated transitions that resemble traditional entry sequences. Architects can minimize these obvious transitions by using solid glass walls and doors, but glass is tricky. Depending upon the light it can either be transparent or act as a mirror.

Ultimately, the transition of entering a building, an essential part of its introduction, can be accomplished in many ways. The Victorian house featured a sequence of entry that began with stepping up to the front porch and concluded with the bang of a screen door. Maybe the field of architecture is ready for a return to that rich experience of entry as a layering of discovery. Picture the small, padded-leather portal of a medieval cathedral, whose dark confines were followed by a spatial explosion into a vast Gothic interior. These small vestibules did more than keep out the weather—they kept the interior a mystery, announcing and accentuating sacred space. But as we now respond to different needs, we must ask contemporary architects to determine a new vocabulary of entry.

Pressure to achieve an interior environment of constant temperature and humidity throughout the year leads to great physical differences between outside and inside, even while transparent glass is used to deny this separation. At the same time, the ceremony of entry has all but disappeared, as guests enter a home through its kitchen and moviegoers flash a smart phone instead of approaching a sales window to purchase a ticket. Nonetheless, there is still the need to define areas of activity and their purposes. The front door may have disappeared from our contemporary architectural language, but the rites and courtesies of entry, so important to previous generations, still hold value. Clarity of movement is essential, and in situations laden with civic symbolism such as the passage across an international border or into a federal courthouse, this experience of entry gains additional significance.

Nineteenth-century architecture's axial views have long been replaced by a geometric frenzy of spatial complexity and startling variety. However, despite architects' manipulations, the multiple routes of entry favored in contemporary architecture can be confusing rather than welcoming. The latter depends upon visitors clearly knowing where they are and how to gain access to the activities they seek. Although directional signage and a blizzard of electronic information are often now available, it is best if a building itself provides orientation. Entry then becomes the first step in an informed and simple journey.

Of the three projects that follow, the New York Botanical Garden welcomes more than six thousand pedestrian visitors on a peak day. The Rainbow Bridge Port of Entry commands an extraordinary site over the Niagara Gorge, offering a symbolic gateway for travelers between the United States and Canada. Multiple points of entry permit the Rainbow Bridge to accept 4.5 million cars and buses each year. The peak population of the recently opened federal courthouse in Jackson, Mississippi, is not yet known, but it is expected to process one hundred trials a year, with bankruptcy hearings and creditor meetings estimated to involve eight hundred to one thousand additional people per year. Each project responds specifically to its location and is designed to provide an entry experience that both welcomes and orients visitors.

New York Botanical Garden
Bronx, New York

As New York City entered the twentieth century, it became America's richest and most ambitious city. Cultural life was influenced by business leaders such as Andrew Carnegie, J.P. Morgan, John D. Rockefeller, and Cornelius Vanderbilt. All these titans were involved in the New York Botanical Garden's creation. They maintained that the burgeoning city needed to be identified by world-class institutions. In 1895, with a $250,000 endowment created by this consortium of New York's wealthiest and most prominent citizens, the garden was launched with an announcement by board president Cornelius Vanderbilt. This new institution was to be noted for upholding the high standards of horticultural, scientific, and educational activities found in its great European counterparts. Influenced by these models (especially the Royal Botanic Gardens at Kew, England), New York City set aside 250 wooded acres of undeveloped land for public use.

Construction of the library building (beginning in 1897) and the conservatory (beginning in 1899) advanced both the scientific and horticultural activities of the garden. The Enid A. Haupt Conservatory, a 520-foot-long glass and cast-iron greenhouse (modeled on the conservatory at Kew), was designed by William R. Cobb of Lord and Burnham. The structure was dominated by an imposing ninety-foot-tall dome. In 1901 the conservatory was ready to receive the public, and a new era of access to nature's wonders began for New Yorkers. The library building, designed by Robert W. Gibson, is a 310-foot-long, 6-story limestone-and-brick structure in the beaux-arts style. Completed in 1901, this library and exhibition hall continues to be the most prominent building at the garden, an expression of its ongoing academic and intellectual mission as a scholarly resource and public research center. In 2002 a fifty-four-thousand-square-foot rear addition was completed by Polshek Partnership to expand the library and herbarium, making this by far the largest building on campus.

When Gregory Long was appointed president in 1989, the garden had fallen deep into neglect. Not only were its gardens ill maintained, its location in the Bronx made people regard it as unsafe. Cars were permitted

Gregory Long
President of the New York Botanical Garden

GL: The visitor's center is really about welcoming visitors and giving them an orientation to the garden. It offers more than just retail or public amenities—it's more about the visitors' whole experience, helping to shape their time at the garden. Our program was very large. We needed thirty thousand square feet to accommodate ticketing, behind-the-scenes visitors' services, locker rooms, the café, the retail shop, and big bathrooms for school groups and bus tours.

This design is tremendously respectful of the historic landscape. Most architects were approaching it as building a thirty-thousand-square-foot building. But Hugh pulled all the pieces apart and created a set of buildings. You don't enter the garden through a structure—you enter the garden through this open courtyard, which has all the structures around to accommodate you. If it's raining or snowing, you dash into the café or the shop. What you need is right there, but it isn't one big monolithic thing.

One of the great things about this visitor's center is that it's OK on a winter day when there are a hundred people here—when there's almost nobody here—and it's fine on a big sunny day if there are ten thousand people here. It can accommodate from a hundred people to ten thousand.

to drive though its pathways, and many visitors felt secure only when viewing nature through their windshields. Long had a simple, revolutionary idea strong enough to transform the place and lead to its financial salvation. He declared it a great museum of plants, one whose collections should be viewed with the same care as objects in any museum. Determined to transform this from being a drive-through museum, he has led a twenty-three-year effort to make the garden pedestrian-friendly, introducing informative signage, trams, and a generous number of benches.

It was only natural for the garden's founders to provide public access by train. Cornelius Vanderbilt was president of the board of managers, and his New York Central Railroad was planning to establish new suburban communities along a rail line up the Harlem Valley. The garden was given its own station, intended to become its front door. More recently, construction of an 825-car parking garage on the west side of the tracks has only increased the importance of this pedestrian entry point.

In 1979 Edward Larrabee Barnes designed a new automotive entrance to the garden, opposite Fordham University, carving out new parking lots. Visitors, after walking through rows of parked cars and buses, would arrive at a dramatic but gloomy gateway in a cyclopean-stone wall that holds back a landscaped berm bridged by a concrete slab. Having entered through a dark tunnel, visitors emerged onto an empty, green lawn. Visual clues like the dome of the conservatory or the great tulip tree axis leading to the library building were out of sight; there was little formal signage, and a confusing variety of paths led to unknown destinations. Instead of feeling inviting, it all seemed mysterious and unwelcoming.

In 2004 the garden asked us to design a new visitor's center, making this more central location a second major entry point to provide expanded access for buses and overflow parking. The authoritative beaux-arts forms of the garden's two major nineteenth-century buildings clearly announce their importance; subsequent structures, however, have been more modest. Creation of a new front door required a design to highlight the significance of this institution. Visitors should recognize the garden's special character as a scientific, educational, and horticultural institution. The architecture should offer an introduction to

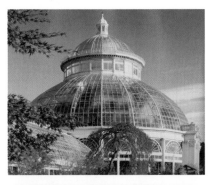

Top Enid A. Haupt Conservatory
Bottom Hemlock Pond

the varied, undulating landscape and acquaint visitors with its access paths and amenities.

The new visitor's center, located inside Barnes's entrance, is both a central vantage point for visitors and a collection of amenities: an orientation area, a ticket booth, a café, toilets, service areas, and a bookstore with a plant shop. Unlike the original empty lawn, this site is generously organized for pedestrians, with maps and general information easily available. Perhaps most important, it creates a sense of arrival. With its new front door, the garden welcomes visitors to unparalleled vistas in a special place.

What would be the appropriate design premise for such a venerable institution? With the exception of Calvert Vaux's exuberant Victorian cottages in Central Park, garden architecture in America has invariably followed a European-influenced classical model. The default idiom for American garden architecture was thus the invention of nobility, reflecting the taste of earlier eras by using a decorative vocabulary borrowed from the European upper classes. For a public garden in New York, however, something more robust seemed appropriate—something made from natural materials and responsive to the site, with all its views and contours. We therefore composed a design that was porous and gentle without any reference to a traditional garden architecture based on the history of other places. We instead offered a design that would show how this progressive institution looks toward the future.

Placement and configuration of the new visitor's center's curving roofs identifies it as a place to discover the landscape. With minimal visible support, each roof offers a sheltering gesture in the form of two horizontal eaves of different heights whose profiles respond to the rolling landscape. This series of pavilions, roofed in six-foot wood deck set upon two-foot-deep laminated wood beams, is supported by four-inch, round, steel columns and stone walls. The columns' thin dimensions are made possible by diagonal stainless-steel braces that lend stability. Generous expanses of glass are positioned to offer sweeping views of the landscape. All of the entrance buildings are joined by wide bluestone walkways that lead to the garden's interior and main circulation paths; the overall design frames the landscape in a series of views that welcome visitors and invite them to explore.

Top Shop in the Garden
Bottom Café

Rainbow Bridge Port of Entry
Niagara Falls, New York

Niagara Falls remains one of the world's natural wonders. It was long the site of daredevil feats in barrels, while passenger trains were suspended over its dramatic gorge containing an astonishing display of water power used to generate electrical energy. The view of double cataracts (165 feet tall on the US side, 159 on the Canadian side) continues to attract an average of twenty-nine-million visitors each year. This historic legacy is now celebrated by the Rainbow Bridge, a single rigid-steel-arched bridge opened just before the attack on Pearl Harbor, in 1941. It continues to be one of the most heavily used border crossings between the United States and Canada. The Rainbow Bridge Authority is a binational private entity with members appointed from both countries. It maintains this access point as well as those nearby at the span over the Whirlpool Rapids and the Lewiston–Queenston Bridge. Together, these three spans serve 7.2 million vehicles annually and are second only to John F. Kennedy International Airport as the most common point of departure for travelers from the United States to Canada.

In 1993 we delivered a successful competition entry to the Rainbow Bridge Authority. The result is a new twenty-six-lane passage between the two countries. Its phased construction required complete demolition of all existing facilities and creation of a totally new experience for public and staff. This major expansion of the border crossing is designed to respond to constant changes in traffic congestion caused by fluctuations in the exchange rate between the two countries' currencies. It must also convey a dignified and welcoming gesture for those entering from Canada and an efficient and pleasant exit for those leaving the United States. The spirit of cooperation between the two countries must be maintained, even as security requirements and inspection procedures have become increasingly complex.

This border-crossing station originally consisted of one- and two-story limestone buildings set in a pattern of curves with a tall lighting tower. This configuration was sufficient for the relatively modest requirements of its time, but subsequent additions made clear the need for a new plan. On the Canadian side, facilities include

Allen Gandell
Former general manager and CEO of the Niagara Falls Bridge Commission

MF: Could you give us a little background on the Rainbow Bridge Authority?

AG: It existed before 1938, but it was reconstituted then through legislation that was passed in that era in order to build the Rainbow Bridge. It was reconstituted as a binational private entity under the auspices of a board that was politically appointed by the governor of the state of New York and the premier of the province of Ontario.

MF: I see. And both entities had to agree on a design?

AG: The design had a lot of pressures and constraints for a lot of different reasons. Let me preface this by saying that I doubt that there would be a more complicated environment in which to try and reach a design that was satisfactory to all parties. It's an international crossing—the number-one land-border crossing for tourism in the United States and Canada. So it's a showcase kind of a project. Further, the utilitarian requirements of immigration and customs are pretty severe.

There are a lot of physical constraints and requirements. Things like the inclusion of an impressive campanile (known to moviegoers from the 1953 thriller film *Niagara* with Marilyn Monroe, who spent the night in its upper bedroom suite). Security was so much less stringent at the time the bridge was built that passports were not even required. The bridge itself could accommodate increasing traffic, but inspection procedures in both countries needed to be improved.

Left Rainbow Bridge toll plaza, 1980s
Right Niagara Falls

Few sites could be more dramatic than the Rainbow Bridge Port of Entry. With a spectacular view of the falls, the steel-arched bridge vaults over the Niagara Gorge to join rocky crags in the rough stone escarpment of both countries. Imbued with all the associations that mark leaving and entering the United States, this is a special place. It was once the site of a wooden railroad trestle that, beginning in 1855, guided steam locomotives over the gorge—a daring feat of engineering inspired by nineteenth-century bravado. It was later the site of a replacement bridge, crushed by winter ice floes in 1938.

Nature is so powerful at this site that it would be foolish to compete. The surroundings of tumbling water, rugged rock, and open sky are so vast that new buildings demand a large, simple gesture, complementary in scale to the bridge. Entry patterns need to be clear both ways, and separate unloading and loading of buses was required. By placing administrative offices and technical functions in a two-story arc over the toll booths, we established a gateway presence, making the stopping point part of a choreographed ritual of arrival. Twenty-six different entry and departure points are collected in

holding cells and the ability to inspect vehicles—anything from cars to very large motor homes and trucks. Because it's an international crossing and it was designated as a navigable waterway, you have to get approval from the coast guard. Because it was a part of a state park, both New York State and the National Park Service of the federal government also had some say in what was done and how it would be done. It involved many political entities and community groups, which were quite strong. When I added it all up, there were something like fourteen or fifteen different agencies of one kind or another, on both sides of the border. The plaza is on the American side, so the majority of them were American.

The environmental-impact study was complex, involving everything from having to relate the height of trees in the park to what people would see from different tourism viewing points to how the building impacts their line of vision. There were all sorts of incredible constraints, and, of course, the bridge commission and the tourism industry first and foremost wanted a showcase piece of architecture that would enhance the tourism experience. This was an attempt to make the bridge an integral part of the tourism experience in Niagara Falls.

MF: Then there's the whole thing about the Falls being a place where newlyweds go on their honeymoon.

AG: Well, not to the extent that it used to be. My dad got married just before he got shipped overseas in World War II, and he honeymooned in Niagara Falls—it was the thing to do. There are still quite a few people who go there to get married.

There were days when lineups to cross the bridge on holiday weekends might stretch for four or five hours. And so the community pressure was enormous on the bridge authority to do something to

a six-hundred-foot-long arc to announce the point of transition between the two countries. The key to design was incorporation of all elements in a large-scale gesture unifying all disparate parts.

Departure from the United Sates provides a deliberately different architectural experience from that of arrival. Facing west, Canada is visible from the Administration Building through vertical, perforated aluminum fins bracketed from the concave elevation to provide shade. The eastern exposure has a convex elevation protected with horizontal patterns of frit glass that recall shutters. The ends of this elegantly detailed two-story main building are set on top of two masonry volumes composed of the same stone as the escarpment. All ground-level structures are set with concealed mortar to resemble a drystone wall. It is the contrast between the polished glass and aluminum shell of the two-story curving building and the rugged stone walls of the support buildings that gives the composition its character.

Contemporary border-crossing inspection often requires investigation of a vehicle as well as its passengers. At its most extreme, this inspection might involve dismantling a vehicle behind closed doors. On the American side of the arc, a large protective canopy covers a two-acre area for these secondary inspections. This canopy is supported by steel columns with an infill of translucent fiberglass sandwich, giving the arc of the building a tail in plan.

Commissioned by the Rainbow Bridge trustees, this project has become a leading example of the work of the US General Services Administration (GSA) Design Excellence Program. Despite the complexity of the project's functions and the need to accommodate wide variations in the number of people processed, the scheme's simple configuration and direct circulation routes are exemplary. It is clearly an important and authoritative gateway for the public. Although not thought of as a destination in its own right, a pedestrian walkway across the Niagara Gorge affords the most dramatic vantage point from which to view both the American and Canadian cataracts.

alleviate congestion. So the goals were very utilitarian: to design a structure to function very well and increase the efficiency of processing; to give Immigration and Customs the tools that they needed to expedite traffic; and somehow to mitigate that congestion. The tourism industry was suffering terribly from the fact that on holiday weekends, for example, people just would not cross the bridge. They were intimidated by the congestion.

So the number-one goal, certainly, was to be able to process that traffic. But you also had to design a structure that the environmental groups, the National Park Service, and the New York State Office of Parks all would consider to be environmentally complementary. They were all very concerned that there would be some negative impact on the natural environment.

MF: Well, apparently the previous bridge collapsed in January 1938 due to an ice dam in the river.

AG: It didn't cost the community a penny; it was totally financed through the issuance of bonds. And so there have never (to my knowledge) been tax dollars used to either build or maintain the bridge.

MF: Why was it decided that there would be a competition instead of simply appointing someone?

AG: We knew in advance how difficult it would be to shepherd a design through all the hurdles and hoops we would have to go through with all the government agencies, and you can't do that unless you have a community strongly behind you, and so we had included prominent members of the community in the process from the very inception. That turned out to be a successful strategy, because at all times, the political and community base was 100 percent behind the project.

United States
Federal Courthouse
Jackson, Mississippi

The basic idea that laws rule behavior and apply to all citizens equally is essential to the functioning of a civilized community. To succeed, our legal system must embody continuity and also accommodate the forces of change. This raises questions about what aesthetic premise should guide the design of a building of the particular prominence and importance of a federal courthouse.

Ever since 1785, when Thomas Jefferson copied a Roman temple (the Maison Carrée in Nîmes, France) for the Virginia State Capitol, classical architecture has served as the basis for American civic buildings. Jefferson hoped to associate the ideals of his own emerging nation with ancient Greek and Roman traditions of democracy and rule by law. Subsequently, a rectangular solid set with a porch of Greek or Roman columns supporting a pediment became the omnipresent style for public architecture, and no region of the United States bears a stronger imprint of this heritage than the South. But is it correct to continue this tradition in the twenty-first century? Is its association with an antebellum society based upon slavery appropriate for contemporary society? Does a classical vocabulary continue to resonate with the public as a representation of respect for the workings of the law?

Prominent buildings designed in the classical style, such as Cass Gilbert's 1935 Supreme Court building in Washington, DC, continue to define the aesthetics of American judicial architecture. However, Roman models cannot accommodate contemporary program needs without distortion or excessive expense. The Jackson, Mississippi, courthouse consists of almost 420,000 square feet of enclosed space. Of that 51 percent is used by administrative staff, 23 percent is open to the public, and 10 percent is designated for the US Marshals; in the nineteenth century, a third as much space might have been sufficient for a courthouse in a city the size of Jackson (population: 170,000). To create a classical hierarchy of columns, cornices, and pediments for a structure of this size and to orchestrate the

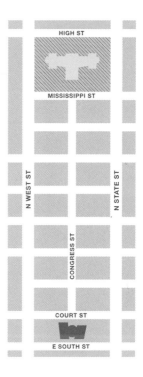

William H. Barbour, Jr.
Senior judge for the Southern District of Mississippi

WB: One of the first things we raised with the architects about the new courthouse was that it should be user-friendly, both for the public and the employees. We were conscious of making this building a facility where the public would feel welcome. Most people entering a courthouse, whether they are litigants, witnesses, jurors, or even lawyers, are apprehensive. We intended to make a building where the general public would be comfortable. An open, friendly building with good signs for directions can greatly relieve some of this anxiety. For instance, we tried to put the jury assembly room in a place that was easily accessible. We were very conscious of trying to make the whole process open, so that members of the public could easily find their way.

Comfortable seating with sufficient lighting and excellent

acoustics also help. We thought that although the building and courtrooms should have dignity and should make a statement of importance, they should not be burdened with unnecessary symbols of authority: dark colors or expressions of legal power. Few people realize how many different workers there are in a courthouse—obviously judges, but many more. All their needs must be accommodated with bright, open spaces that enjoy direct access to sunlight. This diverse population has found that the building works.

Top Mississippi State Capitol
Left United States Federal Courthouse

enormous expanse of decorative detail required to harmonize its giant volumes would demand resources far beyond any contemporary budget.

But even if cost permitted, a classical composition would seem bloated and somewhat comical in the context of twenty-first-century Jackson. The question then arises: What would be the appropriate form for a place in which complex contemporary legal precedents are set? In such a building the public should feel welcome and aware of the present as it relates to tradition rather than as bound by the dogma of the past. The interplay of the law's fixed importance and the flexibility of its ongoing interpretation requires a more thoughtful architectural response than the mindless reproduction of past forms.

Jackson's new courthouse changes the downtown dynamic of this capital city, which is blessed with a magnificent beaux-arts capitol building theatrically set upon a prominent hill facing south. The city's business district lies below, marked by Congress Street, an eight-block-long north–south axis leading from the capitol to the new courthouse. Had the courthouse been organized as a vertical shaft, piling its twelve major courtrooms on top of one another, it would have unfortunately dominated the city's skyline in place of the capitol. Instead, we broke its large bulk into two six-story volumes joined by a central, curving rotunda. Each wing contains six courtrooms, with other administrative offices and government agencies located on the first three floors below. The rotunda is defined by a five-story glass wall whose concave form supplies an architectural response to the capitol's convex dome. At the same time, this glass wall creates a curving gesture of welcome.

Having organized the basic forms, we turned to the question of architectural vocabulary. The glass box—the design premise of the moment—might have been an obvious choice, but a second layer of enclosure for sun control would have been required in Mississippi, making shading devices the major architectural statement and generating an alien appearance in downtown Jackson. Instead we chose precast concrete to enclose the building and provide thermal insulation from the fierce sun. By controlling window size and using solar glass, paying close attention to efficient uses of energy, we hope to secure silver LEED rating (which has not yet been awarded at the time of this writing).

As Daniel Patrick Moynihan's 1962 "Guiding Principles for Federal Architecture" note: "Specific attention should be paid to the possibilities of incorporating into such design[s] qualities which reflect the regional architectural traditions of that part of the Nation in which buildings are located." Our architectural details in Jackson are inspired by vernacular sources. Instead of borrowing architectural traditions from Greece and Rome, we have allied ourselves with more everyday design elements that make this building feel familiar. Harmonious materials, colors, and details used in the courthouse are all directed toward the goal of providing a welcoming environment that encourages participation, not subjugation.

North facade details

Judges' chambers are identified as special through their placement at corners, with trelliswork shading for sun control. Courtrooms are situated in stacks of three in four different locations, and their curving walls are seen through three-story bay windows that animate different facades. Precast concrete panels feature a cast-concrete pattern of overlapping clapboards that resemble the articulations of the region's traditional wooden buildings. Avoiding the slick appearance of glass curtain walls, the rotunda is enclosed with thermal glass randomly patterned with horizontal frit lines to recall the shutters often found on traditional buildings. These are accentuated by a grid of vertical one-story fins made of laminated blue glass (a response to Judge William H. Barbour, Jr.'s enjoyment of the colorful watercolors of local artist Wyatt Waters) contrasted with horizontal aluminum extrusions. Although none of these devices are traditional ornament, as changing shadows move with the angle of the sun they provide the play of light and shade intrinsic to traditional architecture, working to enliven the building's large mass.

Terrorism has created a need to protect ourselves from one another. The design of public buildings is now increasingly involved in matters of security. This vexing situation requires that all public spaces must meet high standards for security, with screening devices a part of the entry sequence for all federal property. Separation of casual visitors from those on official business is no longer possible. Everyone is now inspected, and requirements are constantly changing as new technologies emerge, fostering ever-newer (and always uglier) equipment. Sadly, all this protection limits public access to public buildings.

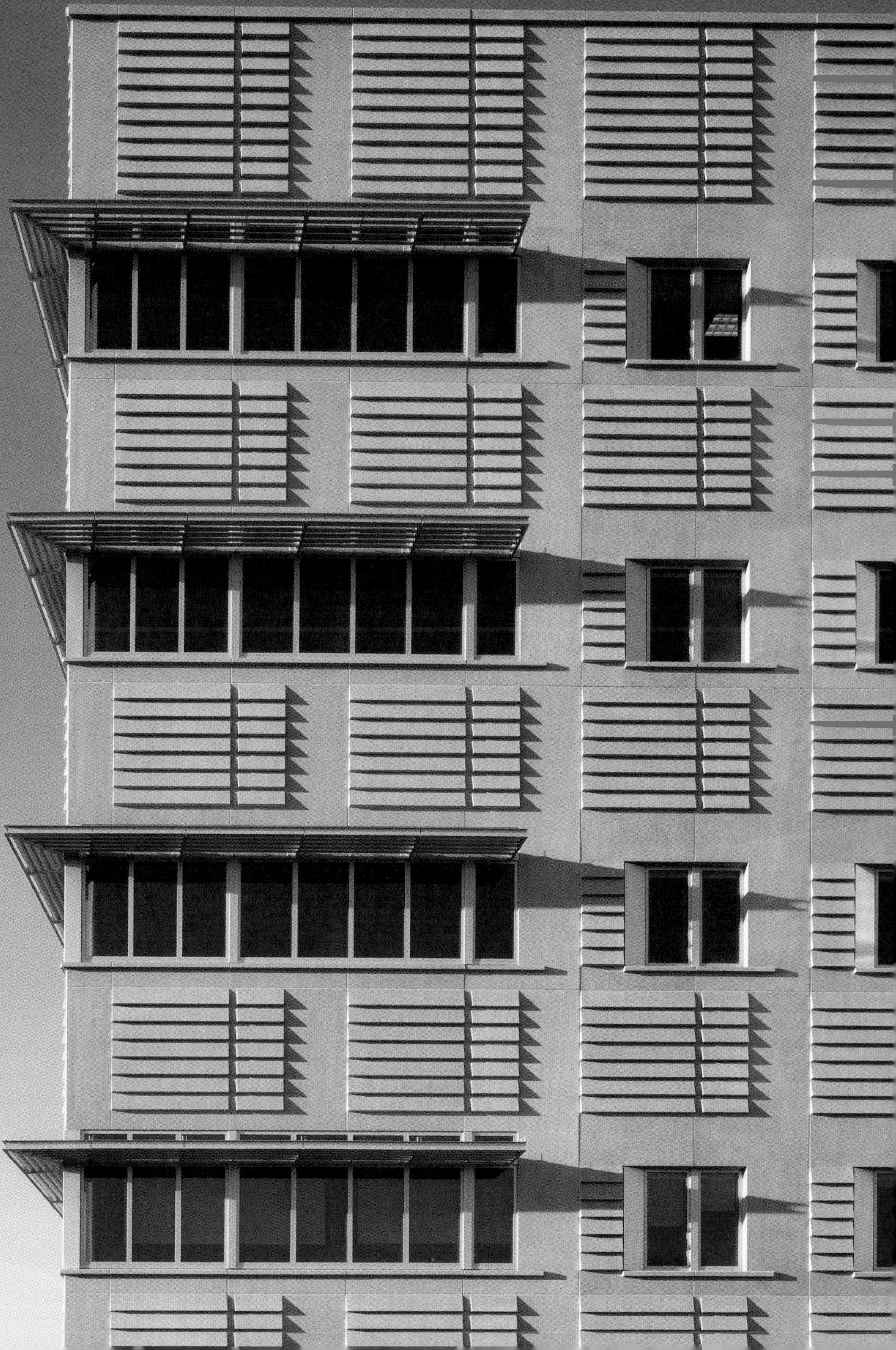

Legend

"Some buildings and places
are so legendary their
reputation overshadows
the reality of their present
physical condition or use."

**New Victory Theater
New York, New York**

Conversations
Cora Cahan
President of the
New 42nd Street

Marian Heiskell
Chair of the New 42nd
Street board of directors

**New Amsterdam Theatre
New York, New York**

Conversation
Rebecca Robertson
Former president
of the 42nd Street
Development Project

"Legend" is concerned with the rebirth
of Forty-Second Street, made possible
by state and local government together
with private enterprise as well as questions
of restoration and reuse presented by
two existing theaters.

Projects

New Victory Theater
New York, New York, restoration in 1995

New Amsterdam Theatre
New York, New York, restoration in 1997

Some buildings and places are so
legendary, their reputation overshadows
the reality of their present physical condition
or use. Forty-Second Street continues to
be one of those places. Before the giant
movie palaces that defined Times Square
in the 1920s extended their dazzling
marquees out over Broadway from Forty-
Second to Fifty-Second Streets, ten live
theaters had transformed a single block
between Broadway and Eighth Avenue,
creating a performance culture that spread
across America. Many communities
built their own Broadway and copied the
form of New York theaters in order to be
eager recipients of New York–produced
entertainment. These road shows taught
Americans how to sing and dance as
well as how to enjoy theater in all its
forms, from classical plays to vaudeville.

A name up in lights was the ticket to an
exuberantly imagined wealth that sometimes
became real. Producers and performers
could make names for themselves that
transcended the boundaries of poverty
and immigrant status. The legend endured,
and even at its lowest point of decay as a
home to dereliction and pornography, Forty-
Second Street was a special address.

Politicians could get into office by promising
to "clean up the Deuce." But after many
false starts, it became obvious that the key
to renewal did not lie in political rhetoric
or office-building development but rather
in the legend itself—if only the theaters
could be brought back to life. Ultimately,
it was a combination of the City and
State of New York in partnership with an
independent nonprofit organization, the
New 42nd Street, Inc., that led to revival.
This strategy involved the type of public-
private partnership long associated
with cultural institutions in New York.

The building that led this revival was the New Victory, reconstructed in 1995 with a program for young audiences, followed by the New Amsterdam, which in 1997 involved the Walt Disney Company in a major act of urban renewal. The presence of the Disney Company, guided by the nonprofit New Victory, lured other investors to a transformed, multiuse Forty-Second Street. With the arrival of Madame Tussauds, Hilton Hotels, a twenty-five-screen AMC movie complex, a multilevel McDonald's, and two corner office buildings, the scale and density of activities on the south side of this block were transformed. To make this possible, the Empire theater was moved 168 feet west, creating space for the hotel and movie theater. The north side contains an equally diverse assortment of entertainment-related activities, following the structural sleight of hand by which two theaters, the Selwyn and the adjacent Times Square theater, were combined to create the American Airlines theater.

Forty-Second Street is once again becoming a destination for family entertainment instead of sleaze. It is a miraculous turnaround for a formerly disgraceful part of the city. Live productions in the New Victory and New Amsterdam theaters affirm the importance of this street as a place dedicated to new ideas in performance. Its current diversity of venues attracts a new variety of visitors appropriate to the "Crossroads of the World." As a result, no two buildings are the same, and each reflects a different attitude about the past. These two theaters follow different economic models; each also embodies its own approach toward restoration, showing alternate ways that new and old can come together. Each of these two transformations represents an exhilarating story of ambition, abandonment, and renewal made possible by the legends of a fabled street.

New Victory Theater
New York, New York

Live performance is an intrinsic form of human expression that none of us can resist. Both children and adults instinctively perform for each other at home or in public. Audiences are everywhere: the dance hall, the campfire, the street, or the cocktail party— all inviting amateur participation. Professional stage presentation elevates skill over simple enthusiasm, but its allure continues to be based upon the basic human need for expression. In New York City, live performance has long been a familiar part of street life, and it is not surprising that it would become the model for live entertainment across America.

The New Victory's revival as a permanent institution not dependent for survival on box-office revenue and Disney's restoration of the New Amsterdam led to an astonishing rush for development across all of West Forty-Second Street as well as the adjacent "bow tie" of Times Square. Each of these reconstructed buildings needed to selectively interpret history in order to operate as functional, code-compliant facilities. Numerous high-tech venues for live contemporary performance now operate in and around Times Square, using techniques and technologies unknown when the original theaters were built; it was the New 42nd Street's sponsorship of the New Victory that led the way. It convinced Michael Eisner, Disney's chairman, that his support for the New Amsterdam would happily lead to more than a single restored theater standing in a wasteland.

Forty-Second Street's reign as New York's premier theater district began in 1899 with Oscar Hammerstein's construction of the Victoria theater and roof garden at the corner of Broadway and Forty-Second Street. Over the years a collection of new halls grew into the greatest concentration of legitimate theaters of any city in America. Ten were eventually located on each side of this single midtown block, and by the 1927–1928 season, there were more than seventy theaters in the Times Square area. Productions that originated here played coast to coast.

In 1900 Hammerstein built the elegant Republic theater next door to his Victoria, with a traditional two-balcony opera-house plan supported by

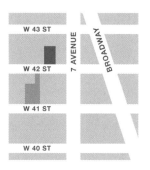

Cora Cahan
President of the New 42nd Street

CC: If you're talking to an architect by the end of a construction project, it's really a rare thing— rare and unique. Because if you are a good client, you get involved. If you're not a good client, you don't get involved. The best outcomes that come out of building or making something new come from having a dynamic, informed, involved client in a tug-of-war with the not-so-necessarily pragmatic— meaning that you know what you need. The architect is not going to know that you like to turn on the light switch three inches from the floor with your toe. (I'm making that up!) So the best outcomes are when there's a real dialogue, in the best sense—pushing and pulling to the next level—and maybe even an argument.

As far as Marian Heiskell (the chair of the board) and I were concerned, Hugh was the person to take this 1900 theater and bring it back and restore it in a way that would honor its past and still make it an appropriate venue where young people—kids, nine-year-olds— would be happy. And not make it primary colors—yellow, red, and blue—because, actually, that would have been appalling, and it would have been wrong. You can't take a jewel-box theater and suddenly make it into a kiddie theater, and we weren't going to do kiddie stuff on the stage. And so we made it, with Hugh's help, into this beautiful restoration and reinvention.

decorative cast-iron columns. Distinguished by a double-staircase entrance, the Republic first prospered but was sold after two years to David Belasco (the dynamic, imaginative producer who later gave us *Show Boat*). After a few indifferent years it became the home to *Abie's Irish Rose*, at one time the longest-running show on Broadway. When burlesque became popular, Billy Minsky took over the theater, removed the front staircases, and offered the only show in town with double runways built out into the auditorium. Subsequently, as its elaborate interior slowly sank into decay, the theater became a home for second-run movies. By the early 1970s it survived by showing pornography all day long to an audience of lonely men in raincoats.

Left Original facade of the Republic, circa 1900

Right Exterior decay, circa 1990

With the collapse of live entertainment under the onslaught of movies as well as television and other home-entertainment devices, this block of Forty-Second Street was left with ten moldering buildings that had either been abandoned or were showing second-run movies and porn. Eventually, under Governor Hugh Carey and Mayor Edward Koch, the State and City of New York took control of these buildings. A special entity, the 42nd Street Development Corporation, was created to undertake the restoration and reconstruction of the theaters for entertainment uses. In 1984 the Municipal Board of Estimate approved a renewal plan with the establishment of an independent government agency charged with leasing each building to a different private institution and returning them to profitability, preferably through staging live performance.

I was running a ballet company and the Joyce theater in 1988 and 1989, and the city and state were dealing with this street. They approached me and the Joyce about whether any of the theaters on Forty-Second Street could become a dance theater. I was again approached and asked, early in 1990, if I would consider leaving the dance world and coming and dealing with these seven or eight potential theaters on Forty-Second Street.

The idea of a kids' theater was probably the last thing on my mind, and if anyone had said "kids' theater," I would have said that we don't do them. We can't afford to do them: you can't subsidize them, you have to have low ticket prices, you would have to have an education program.

There was no operating money, but there was renovation money from the developers of the corners at Forty-Second Street and Broadway. The developers of those buildings were required to provide up to 18.2 million dollars to renovate two theaters for nonprofit uses.

It was irresponsible to bring anybody to this blighted block. No office buildings were going up—those developers were going away. And so we said: OK, we have nothing to risk. What can we do that will fill a cultural void in the city's fabric (which has so many really superb cultural organizations) that is not being filled by anybody else? We don't want to tread on anybody else's territory.

Theatre for a New Audience was doing shows for kids in this cold, damp, ugly Victory. Ugly and rundown. Not ugly, but rundown. In January of 1991, one month after the board had its first meeting, I took a look at the school buses on the block. There was nothing else on the block but sex shops. And the kids from those public schools were looking down at this drab theater with broken-down seats and not enough heat and the women in costumes like Juliet dresses with their breasts pushed up. They were sitting in the balcony looking down, totally intrigued by *Romeo and Juliet*. Once we said

In 1990 the 42nd Street Development Corporation created the New 42nd Street, Inc., with Cora Cahan as president, preferring to put the theaters back to work rather than sponsoring high-rise office towers in a part of town where there was no market. To avoid the boom-or-bust finances of commercial theater, nonprofit status was established for what was then still known as the Republic, where porno movies were still being shown. The use of a public-private partnership has many New York precedents, and in this case it led to an astonishing physical and cultural transformation. The street's visible change began with restoration of the Republic, renamed the New Victory. With its commitment to presenting an annual agenda of performers from all over the world to young audiences and offering subsidized tickets and program connections to New York City schools, this institution would not be dependent solely upon box-office revenues.

Imagine the strength of character to announce redemption of this derelict theater on a dangerous street as a place where young audiences could discover the magic of live performance! Under the aegis of the New 42nd Street, Inc., the New Victory established a board of directors and inaugurated its nonprofit program. These would not be "children's theater" presentations; the board invited performers from around the world: acrobats, dancers, storytellers, and mimes of great variety and sophistication. The result has been theater unlike any in New York, all taking place in this small, beautifully transformed two-balcony opera house.

Restoration of the New Victory required awareness of its varied former aesthetic approaches and uses. Hammerstein had originally designed an embellished interior with a tall proscenium sporting an upper musicians' balcony. When Belasco rebuilt the interior two years later, he increased stage depth and rigging for scenery. Later, when Minsky removed the front staircases, he added a marquee, gaudy signage, and ornate lobby plasterwork to give the place a more "high-class French" appearance for his burlesque shows. Eventually, as Forty-Second Street was widened for cars and trolleys, the use of the rooftop for performances ceased.

Which "original" appearance should be restored? The entrance staircases seemed the most important element. Replacement of the cornice was next, but reconstruction of the original rooftop arcade and urns

Stage view of the theater

"kids' theater," the board said the risk of not going ahead with the New Victory was greater than the risk of going ahead. There was no model for what we were doing: there was no basis; there was no revenue; there was no way to support it. So we went around the world and came back with the idea of finding good work and presenting it on the stage— being a presenting house rather than creating the work.

Marian Heiskell
Chair of the New 42nd Street board of directors

MH: People said, "A children's theater in New York?" I remember Kitty Hart, who was on our committee, said, "That's ridiculous. You can't bring children into a place like this!" And Charles Platt said, "Of course you can. I've been bringing my children down to Broadway on this street for years."

And then Kitty calls me up after we'd started and says, "I was wrong, Marian. This is really wonderful." And the present theater is such a change from that shabby-looking thing. It was hard to imagine it would become so magical.

was not financially feasible or intrinsically required by the new program. They were replaced to much greater effect by a large neon rooftop sign accompanied by other code-mandated neon blade signage and borders.

But what to do about the interior design? Should we return to Hammerstein's decor? This would cause—after demolition—considerable expense, require reference to photography of questionable accuracy, and be less authentic than the portions of the interior that remained from other eras. We ultimately kept Belasco's plasterwork and interior design, although, oddly, when he changed the interior he had removed lyres from the cupids surrounding the dome. Was this to avoid the link with music and opera? In any case, we decided these *putti* needed their lyres back. Finding one in the attic to use as a sample, we recast and replaced all eight. For further accuracy, we avoided the false mosaic stenciling used by Hammerstein in the ribs of the ceiling dome in favor of Belasco's color scheme and faux drapery for the walls. The seats are all new, with updated profiles and aisle standards as well as upholstery that uses a pattern of bees (often used as an emblem of Belasco). The carpet is a smaller-scale version of the flowered pattern used in the lobby and gives appropriate scale and color to the aisles.

Sightlines from the second balcony seating had previously been compromised unless patrons leaned forward, and they often put their feet on the backs of the seats in front of them, providing a poor example of behavior for young audience members. The upper balcony was therefore rebuilt with wider back-to-back seat spacing in three rows, giving full views to audience members on all levels. New basement access to the lower lobby mandated a fire separation between the auditorium and the lobby. This was achieved with fire doors and a new wall at the back of the auditorium on three levels that also helps to baffle sound from Forty-Second Street. Although it is a new architectural element, it is covered with appropriately figured and textured fabric reflective of nineteenth-century taste.

By today's standards, the original theater had totally inadequate toilet facilities and absurdly small dressing rooms. Locating toilets in a new sidewalk vault space required a stair to a new lower lobby level excavated under and around the existing structure. Space for a concession stand could then be tucked under the existing orchestra seating. These amenities for the audience were matched by backstage facilities housed

Top Box detail
Bottom Upper box
Opposite View of proscenium

in an adjoining building. An elevator necessary
for wheelchair access to all levels required a new
vertical shaft. It was accommodated through major
insertions in the original building that make no
attempt to look original.

Some might bemoan the inaccuracy of this
restoration, finding it unfaithful to history. Instead,
I believe it is historically accurate because it speaks
of the building's many lives over the ninety-five
years preceding its restoration. The historical
context of this public place is as important as its
various physical elements. So much has changed
on Forty-Second Street that even if it were possible,
an accurate restoration of what this building once
was—in any period—would be neither code-compliant
nor functional. Restoration becomes increasingly
impure the farther back in time its sources lie, and
those engaged in this activity must identify which
parts of the building's story are worth telling and
which can be ignored. It becomes, therefore, a
highly subjective rather than a scientific activity.

The New Amsterdam was conceived by Klaw & Erlanger, a powerhouse team of early twentieth-century Broadway producers. Their 1903 theater was more resplendent than any other on Forty-Second Street. In 1979 it was declared a landmark, but by the 1980s, the theater stood devastated. The main support columns were left open to the elements after an incomplete investigation of its steel structure. Sustained by leaks in the roof, mushrooms grew on the orchestra floor.

The theater had been built by Marcus Klaw and A. L. Erlanger to be their most significant architectural achievement, its main 2,100-seat hall constructed for spectacle with an uncommonly large stage. But their initial production of *A Midsummer Night's Dream* was an overproduced box-office failure, and few subsequent productions were successful until Florenz Ziegfeld, Jr., made it his home for the Ziegfeld Follies in 1913. Above the main auditorium was a second theater, reached by elevator, that originally featured flexible seating and glass window walls that looked out over the surrounding city. There *The Midnight Frolic* was staged for the delight of those who sought risqué nightlife. While frankly commercial in intent, the New Amsterdam was also built for quality of experience, with amenities rare for the period and a dedication to artistic surroundings that represented a growing desire for luxury in the middle class.

By 1982 the New Amsterdam had become a scene of ruin. Its two stacked theaters, each with a glorious history, had both suffered abandonment. One quadrant of the ceiling in the main hall had collapsed, decorative plasterwork was missing or decomposing, seating boxes had been removed for film projection, and some murals were falling off or had disappeared. The seats were gone and three feet of water filled the basement. So much plaster had fallen that it was impossible to use the stairwells. Although the rooftop theater retained its stage, its roof leaked, its rigging was unusable, and its interior was stripped of all furnishings. The main theater's entrance lobby had lost its lighting fixtures and a faux-stained-glass painted ceiling had been shattered. Almost every surface needed to be replaced.

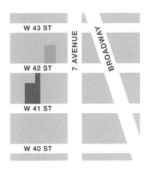

Rebecca Robertson
Former president of the 42nd Street Development Project

MF: Why was Disney such an important factor in the rebirth of Forty-Second Street?

RR: We needed an entertainment tenant with real credibility to convince the world that the new plan for Forty-Second Street—which combined art, entertainment, tourism, and commerce—was viable financially and could succeed. Even though the actual frontage of the New Amsterdam theater on the eight-hundred-foot-long block of Forty-Second Street between Broadway and Eighth Avenue was just twenty feet, its impact in convincing investors, politicians, and the public that Forty-Second Street was no longer the Deuce was astounding.

MF: Why did Michael Eisner so strongly support the project?

RR: He was brought to the New Amsterdam by his board member Robert A. M. Stern, who was also one of the architects of the 42nd Street Development Project's critically acclaimed 1992 plan for the block. Disney was just entering the Broadway producing business (which they have done with great success) and did not want to be subject to the major theater owners who controlled all of the Broadway houses. They wanted their own house. The "New Am" had been at one time the best of the houses and the home of the famed Ziegfeld

<u>Left</u> Original facade of the New Amsterdam, 1925
<u>Right</u> Interior decay in 1992

However, the quartered oak paneling of the auditorium walls for the most part remained, albeit considerably darkened with age and losing the original greenish cast mentioned in contemporary accounts. A large proscenium mural depicted allegorical figures set in a fantasy forest. The central seated figure, Poetry, is flanked by Truth, whose foot crushes Falsehood. Tradition, standing at her other side, holds a scroll. In addition, a glorious mottled-green terra-cotta handrail led to the mezzanine. Despite the many indignities suffered by the interiors, we could use these clues as guides to colors and finishes for the restoration. But they were not enough to determine what the relative brightness of the colors should be or how to modulate them into a coherent whole. A lucky find was an original terra-cotta light fixture saved in an upper storage room that clearly identified the colors and values of the interior walls. It featured Aurora, goddess of the dawn, imagined as a reluctant maiden with light bulbs in her hair. In addition, the large proscenium mural, although partially repainted by Ziegfeld to make its standing figure Truth a more dramatic and buxom nude, still displayed its original color configuration and could be used to guide overall hue and value selection.

An autumnal palette was generally used throughout to complement the proscenium mural. Seating upholstery, carpets, and a new house curtain were designed in the spirit and colors of the original designs, using contemporary descriptions and historic black-and-white photography. Our intent was to give the theater the appearance of a grand old lady, respected and cared for, not to re-create her appearance when a child.

Follies, and had a high seat count. Mr. Eisner obviously believed that the street could be turned around, in which case he would have the best theater in the best location. He was also a New Yorker and wanted to contribute to bringing back Times Square to the great populist public space it had once been.

MF: Has the presence of Disney enhanced or diminished New Yorkers' affection for Forty-Second Street?

RR: If the number of visitors is an indication, Forty-Second Street is vastly more loved than it has ever been. For those who admired the grit of the Deuce, Disney has probably diminished their affection for the street. But beneath that seemingly louche grit was a world of daily tragedy—runaways with AIDS, drug deals gone violent, underage prostitution, and child exploitation. In its heyday, Forty-Second Street was very populist. It is that again. What could be more populist than Disney?

The original facade had boasted a four-story embellishment consisting of poster boxes, doubled columns, and a one-story arch topped by allegorical sculptural figures (whose symbolism is now lost). All this featured increasingly elaborate signage but no true marquee. When in 1937 policies shifted from live performance to the movies, the facade was updated by stripping off its sculptural ornamentation and replacing it with a tall art-deco shaft that sported blinking neon bands. In a second alteration, these were surmounted by a clock and an illuminated marquee lobby cantilevered over the sidewalk. This dazzling addition newly proclaimed that this was now a theater befitting the movies. At the same time a resplendent art-deco terrazzo floor was added that linked the sidewalk box office to new single-pane glass front doors featuring vertical, cylindrical glass handles.

The New York State Historic Preservation Office originally asked us to restore the facade based upon black-and-white photography, but the New York City Landmarks Preservation Commission had made the existing facade a landmark. Negotiations ensued in which arguments for the greater authenticity of the existing composition gained sway, and we compromised by retaining the marquee and clock but removing pink mirrored-glass panels in the lobby that had been set below plasterwork tableaux of scenes from Shakespeare's best-known plays. Like its companion theater, the New Victory across the street, the New Amsterdam embodies history through an amalgam of design features of different eras.

The Rooftop Theater, located above the movie auditorium and home to Ziegfeld's *Midnight Frolic*, could not be restored. Not only had the surrounding city grown up to block out the once-glorious nighttime views through its two-story glass walls, the high-energy sound of contemporary productions on the main stage could not be isolated from this rooftop perch. Furthermore, the elevators originally put in place to serve this small upper hall were now used by the patrons of the large hall below, making simultaneous access to both unworkable. The bones of this room where Ziegfeld had developed young talent amid late-night revelry and the memories of its fame for radio broadcasts still exist, but except for an occasional rehearsal, it remains an unused rooftop relic at the center of Forty-Second Street.

<u>Top</u> Aurora light fixture
<u>Bottom</u> Lobby

Place

"The sense of place in
Cooperstown is so
powerful that it directly
influences contemporary
architectural expression."

**Fenimore Art Museum
Cooperstown, New York**

Conversations
Eugene Thaw
Donor of the Eugene and
Clare Thaw Collection at
the Fenimore Art Museum

Kent Barwick
Former president of the
Municipal Art Society of
New York and former
chair of the New York City
Landmarks Preservation
Commission

**National Baseball
Hall of Fame
Cooperstown, New York**

Conversation
Jane Forbes Clark II
President of the
Clark Foundation

This chapter is concerned with a specific place: Cooperstown, New York, and two museums located there—examples of my response to the existing context of this historic village.

Projects

Fenimore Art Museum
Cooperstown, New York, additions in 1995

National Baseball Hall of Fame
Cooperstown, New York, 2005

Some special places combine so much beauty and history they are unlike any other. Cooperstown, New York, is not only blessed with a rolling agricultural landscape, undisturbed forestland, handsome Greek-revival farmhouses, a nostalgia-provoking nineteenth-century Main Street, and proud civic structures, it also enjoys an uncommon history. Cooperstown was named in honor of James Fenimore Cooper, an early chronicler of Native Americans. His series *The Leatherstocking Tales* was published from the 1820s through the 1840s for an enraptured literary public. These novels, set in Cooperstown, form a dramatic tale of American pioneers in conflict with American Indians.

Cooperstown is set between undulating hills at the bottom of the eight-mile-long Lake Otsego (headwaters of the Susquehanna River), whose surface reflections are constantly changing color, making lakeside views as important a part of village character as its buildings. Its original Main Street is now dominated by tourists and baseball memorabilia, due to the National Baseball Hall of Fame's location there.

It is also home to the Clark family, of Singer Sewing Machine wealth, with Jane Clark representing its fifth generation's continuing presence in the affairs of the town. Edward C. Clark, the fortune's founder, was a patron of architecture, commissioning the French-inspired family seat, Fernleigh, in 1869; it still regally stands in stone-walled splendor. He built a number of other family mansions in New York City, as well as the luxurious apartment house the Dakota, designed by Henry J. Hardenbergh and completed in 1884. (Clark had previously commissioned Hardenbergh to design the Kingfisher Tower on Lake Otsego in 1876, in the intention of beautifying the lake and gracing America with European picturesque embellishment.) Ernest Flagg, a friend of Edward, was retained by the Singer Corporation to design New York City's Singer Building in 1908 and the colonnaded Cooperstown Art Association building.

Cooperstown currently has an unusually diverse civic life, particularly in summer. It enjoys two country clubs, a fine hospital, numerous boating activities, and several museums and historic houses, all presided over by the five-story brick-and-stone Otesaga Hotel, commissioned in 1909 by Edward Severin Clark (grandson of Edward C. Clark). The nearby Farmers' Museum has assembled several eighteenth-century buildings in an imagined town setting next to a great stone barn designed by Frank Whiting in 1917. It displays the tools and techniques that fostered agriculture before the age of the machine, together with the products of numerous other crafts such as weaving and basketmaking. The town is also home to the acclaimed National Baseball Hall of Fame, founded by Edward Severin Clark's brother Stephen C. Clark, which attracts more than 350,000 visitors a year to Cooperstown, including a deluge of attendees for its annual inauguration rites. The New York State Historical Association, founded in 1899, operates a private library open to scholars and the public. Each of these museums offers changing exhibitions and welcomes a wide range of public activities throughout the year.

All these institutions are housed in buildings that respond to their purposes and their surroundings. The Fenimore Art Museum was originally a private house built for Edward Severin Clark on the west shore of Lake Otsego. The museum offers a program of changing exhibitions made possible by additions and alterations completed by my firm in 1995. It also houses the Eugene and Clare Thaw Collection of American Indian Art, whose delicacy and beauty are internationally known.

On Main Street, the National Baseball Hall of Fame occupies 97,500 square feet of space and represents an amalgam of seven different buildings constructed from 1939 to 2005. Here, our greatest challenge was to clarify a circulation route that would make a visit to its exhibitions stimulating rather than fatiguing. This needed to be accomplished without overshadowing the museum's neighboring small-scale nineteenth-century architecture.

As these projects show, the sense of place in Cooperstown is so powerful that it directly influences contemporary architectural expression (focusing design explorations on interiors). The long, skillfully managed continuity of its built environment forms a basic part of the town's identity. Even though no two buildings are the same, their scale and visual vocabulary respond to town-planning and decorative traditions that exert a calm authority. To cause a break in this time-honored vocabulary with aggressive new design ideas would clearly be alien; the results would call more attention to the architect than to the place.

The Eugene and Clare Thaw Gallery

Fenimore Art Museum
Cooperstown, New York

Located on the western shore of Lake Otsego, this museum was originally sponsored by the New York State Historical Association, dedicated to the early history of New York. Although the association dates back to 1899, the Fenimore Art Museum (originally the Fenimore House Museum) was launched in 1944 when Stephen C. Clark, Edward C. Clark's grandson, gave the museum his late brother Edward Severin Clark's house to found a new institution. The museum was established with a collection of paintings, bronze busts of important historical figures, and regional folk art. Open only in summer months, the house could not provide a first-class museum environment and served a loyal but limited population.

In 1995 the Clark Foundation accepted a rare gift, the Eugene and Clare Thaw Collection of American Indian Art, to be housed in an eighteen-thousand-square-foot addition. Consisting of more than 860 objects, this is one of America's finest collections of art. It is especially appropriate that it found a home here, given the early history of Cooperstown's Native American population. The simple beauty and fanciful patterning of masks, clothing, weapons, and ritual objects made of fragile natural materials—feathers, skins, fur, and thread—both surprise and inform a growing public. Presented in natural wood casework with fiber-optic lighting designed by Stephen Saitis, the installation offers an exceptionally sophisticated setting for an outstanding collection.

We enlarged this once-modest local museum and upgraded its facilities to those of a first-class institution. To avoid encroaching on a pastoral lake setting, we expanded the museum underneath adjacent sloping land, transforming a former indoor swimming pool into new gallery space with an extension of the existing garden terrace above. New exhibition, support, service, administration, and auditorium spaces were tucked under this new landscape. The entire facility was then given a temperature and humidity control system that fulfills the exhibition criteria of the American Association of Museums, permitting the museum to accept objects on loan from other

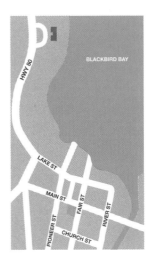

Eugene Thaw
Donor of the Eugene and Clare Thaw Collection at the Fenimore Art Museum

ET: The Fenimore Art Museum had a very strong, very famous folk-art collection given to them by Stephen Clark, the great painting collector. Stephen Clark gave the collection and the building that became the Fenimore Art Museum.

It has his collection of old paintings and American folk art and furniture and things of the nineteenth century. It was a landmark museum and one of the glories of Cooperstown.

The new galleries are one of the iconic spaces for American Indian art anywhere in the world. There's no place else where you can see it as clearly and as beautifully installed as in Cooperstown.

At the time that I was building the collection, someone estimated that I bought a piece every three days for ten years. And I wasn't just trying to buy average pieces. I tried to get things that could be classified as masterpieces of art rather than just proof of how Indians did things—how they made pots or belt-hooks. They had to

certified institutions and greatly expanding the scope of its year-round exhibition program.

The museum's front entrance has always been clearly identified by a two-story portico centered on its west elevation. Once inside, visitors ascend by elevator or stair to the second floor or descend to the new lower galleries. Transition from the residential scale of the original house to the large gallery space below that presents the Thaw collection involves a shift in orientation, scale, and character. The gallery's entrance lobby lies at the foot of a great double stair. At its landing, the lower level comes partially into view as part of an unexpected sequence of discovery. The central gallery is supported by solid limestone columns set beneath clearly visible concrete beams. These big, abstract forms offer a formal contrast to the small-scale Georgian ornament found in the house above.

Fenimore Art Museum garden terrace

An auditorium seating 121, a study center, and amenities for staff and public are also found at the gallery level. A service tunnel with receiving space for art objects is tucked into the grassy hill. Set on the expanded landscaped terrace, a small café offers handsome views of Lake Otsego framed by two small, symmetrical garden pavilions that provide sheltered seating. The museum was expanded without altering the building's basic character or profile, since only a small portion of the modest new exterior walls are visible from the outside. The new garden terrace thus integrates old and new, displaying a balanced architectural composition.

be supreme examples of art— as good as tribal art anywhere.

Every year they rearrange a lot of the cases and add pieces. At least two-thirds of the collection is in the study center. There's a so-called open storage area, where you can see the rest of the collection. They're not the poorer pieces; they're good pieces—or as good as the ones that are on display—and we change them around once in a while and put some of the pieces from the study collection into the main galleries and vice-versa.

You can look at the pieces in the study collection right on the table where you're working— you can actually have contact with the object.

The museum presents an overall survey of American Indian work arranged by geographic area. So you walk in and start with the Northeast—the woodlands area—and then you go on and see the Eskimo and Northwest Coast areas, and then around the next corner is the Southwest area with Navajo blankets and pots, and then you come to the Plains, with the beadwork and quillwork and feathers and shields and horse trappings. It's a tremendously lucid installation.

Probably the strongest and most important section is the Northwest Coast, where we have these unbelievably early and great carvings going back to Captain Cook's time and even earlier.

So in the effort to get masterworks, we bought as much as we could find in auctions and in Europe. A lot of the greatest material came from castles and country houses in England, because the aristocracy (the younger sons) used to come to America to hunt and to establish a career. And they would send back great Indian material that would just go in chests in their attics. They thought that it was a dying culture and that they had better save it, whereas the Americans thought they were vermin and destroyed everything. It wasn't until the Smithsonian Institution began to save some things in the late nineteenth century that

Eugene and Clare Thaw Collection of American Indian Art

we collected it at all; it was the European nobility and some of the fur traders who saved some of this material. Also, if you put it in a trunk in the attic of your castle, it didn't get destroyed by moths the way most of it did here.

The ensemble includes the Indian wing and this unbelievable terrace on top. If you're a contemplative person and you want to meditate, that's the place to go.

We sometimes have other loan shows, and we use the central hall often for those exhibitions. So there's a great flexibility that Hugh has built into it.

There's a smaller gallery under the great staircase, which we use for smaller shows. We put out our best baskets there one year. Another year we hung the Navajo weavings, and another year we put out the prints of Edward Curtis photographs.

When the museum opened, we had a celebration with Indian speakers. We had some great chiefs of the Mohawk and the Onandaga tribes come to give blessings. The Iroquois Indian nation is pretty militant and feels it has gotten a raw deal, like so many Indians have, so we thought there would be some trouble. But on the contrary, we were surprised by the reaction. One critic said that by putting our collection up as great art, we showed respect, and that was what they were looking for: respect. And they love us now.

Current art-museum fashions mandate large areas of glass. But in this instance the type of aggressive, new transparent addition customary for the display of large-scale, contemporary art was fortunately not called for, since the Thaw collection requires subdued light to protect its fragile materials, and the museum's other collections are also light sensitive. Natural light is therefore excluded from the main galleries. By deliberately setting the museum into its hillside, with only the central gallery opening to a view of the lake and no skylights, we could add gallery space that uses only fiber-optic lighting in its display areas. Always distinctive, this large house has now been transformed sensitively into a professional museum.

The opening day in 1995 featured a sky resplendent with lowering thunderclouds. The new galleries were inaugurated by Chief Jake Swamp, a spiritual leader of the Mohawk Nation, who spoke of the sacred connection between this site and the objects in the museum. Suddenly, amid the rumblings of thunder, he was dramatically washed with sunbeams as he gave stirring testimony to Cooperstown's Indian heritage and the power of art. Now, a thirty-foot-tall totem pole, gift of Eugene and Clare Thaw, stands before the museum, signifying the connection between its collections and the Indian legacy of Cooperstown.

Kent Barwick
Former president of the Municipal Art Society of New York and former chair of the New York City Landmarks Preservation Commission

KB: Fenimore House was a wonderful building, a private house that had been owned by Edward Severin Clark on the grounds of a farm that had belonged to James Fenimore Cooper. There wasn't a lot left from the James Fenimore Cooper era except a great allée of trees, which went down from the side of the house

<u>Top</u> Main gallery
<u>Bottom</u> Central stair

to the lake. The house that he built, which went with those wonderful barns across the street (the Farmers' Museum), had a big terrace, and I think underneath the terrace was a swimming pool.

His brother (Jane Clark's grandfather, Stephen C. Clark) was a great collector of all kinds of art; his collection is the basis of the Metropolitan Museum of Art's impressionist collection. He invited the New York State Historical Association to come to Cooperstown to set up headquarters in Fenimore House. At that point, the swimming pool was converted into a gallery. But they didn't spend a lot of money on it—they just took the water out and put some sheetrock over the walls.

It was a great place. It was run with great imagination by a succession of directors, some of whom were very prominent, and they began to collect American art. They initially bought Hudson River School paintings, and they bought a wonderful collection of life masks of prominent figures, made in the early eighteenth century through a process that is now lost but involved pouring wax over people's faces for long periods of time. Thomas Jefferson almost suffocated; he didn't like the experience. But some of the life masks are real likenesses of prominent persons. They then began buying American folk art. This was taking place in the 1950s, but then the organization began to stand pat. It wasn't that they weren't doing first-class work, but they didn't continue that dynamic growth. They had had wonderful collections, and they started a graduate program in museum training, and they had the oldest history quarterly on the East Coast. But then along came Gene and Clare Thaw. And Gene and Clare have assembled an extraordinary collection of American Indian art.

National Baseball Hall of Fame
Cooperstown, New York

Stephen C. Clark established the National Baseball Hall of Fame in 1939; it has since grown to include seven buildings on Main Street in Cooperstown. Based around the legend that the game of baseball began with Abner Doubleday at Cooperstown's modest stadium, the Hall of Fame now attracts more than 350,000 visitors annually. The quintessential American sport, baseball generates a blizzard of statistics and ephemera. Exhibition material is artfully displayed to preserve game scores and programs; players' numbers, uniforms, and equipment; autographed bats and balls; life-size images of personalities like Babe Ruth and Jackie Robinson; and illustrations of various major-league ballparks. Each year, new Hall of Famers are inducted into the chapel-like hall at the center of the museum—a cause for major celebration. With more than 35,000 miscellaneous artifacts, 130,000 baseball cards, and 26,000,000 library items, this is a leading cultural destination for people from all over the country.

The museum's expansive growth had compromised the internal logic of its original structures. Built over time, its seven different buildings were stylistically similar but separately organized. Mechanical systems were patched together, inefficient, and inadequate. Circulation was unwieldy and seemingly endless; visitors were often more confused than enlightened by their visits, and reconstruction was called for.

On the exterior, a modified Georgian facade had undergone several revisions using matching materials and details. In fact, the facade's 182-foot-long masonry expanse has nothing to do with sports or a baseball stadium's design—it is a direct expression of Stephen Clark's architectural taste. At the same time, a violent contemporary architectural gesture would now be no more welcome on Main Street than a titanium-and-glass baseball with its stitches made of some luminescent space-age material. Our greatest challenge was to clarify the facility's circulation while remaining respectful of the small scale of Cooperstown's nineteenth-century architecture. Therefore, with the exception of moving one exterior wall toward

Jane Forbes Clark II
President of the Clark Foundation

JFC: I am president of the Clark Foundation. The entire family has an enormous interest still in the preservation of Cooperstown as a wonderful place to live. Our advertising theme is "America's Perfect Village." Even more, we are very interested in the well-being of the community and the people who live there. We provide advice and management oversight to all of those institutions we call Clark affiliates.

They are all involved in Cooperstown. We have a sports center, an elder-care facility, two hotels, a resort golf course, three museums, two foundations. And we also provide nine hundred—almost a thousand—scholarships a year to graduating high school students from the Cooperstown school district and the nine surrounding school districts. So we do a lot.

The Baseball Hall of Fame is a huge drawing card to Cooperstown. The Farmers' Museum and the Fenimore Art Museum—their attendance is fifty, sixty thousand a year.

the street to gain space for a new three-story hall and the addition of a glass clerestory, almost all our renovations were deliberately internal and required no visible exterior alterations.

By completely reorganizing the internal circulation routes, we created a circular movement pattern that logically recurs on each floor. Movement was dramatized throughout with the use of glass handrails and quiet finishes, using no complex details, and we inserted a three-story monumental stair to connect all four floors. Even though the combined exteriors of the Hall of Fame's various buildings reflect the donor's original and consistent architectural taste, we found little reason to constrain the stair hall's interior design to the gentle Georgian vocabulary of the exterior. This chamber, filled with natural light from a clerestory above, offers a welcome break from the density of exhibits.

Visiting the Hall of Fame is an important pilgrimage for those who love baseball. Although not distinguished in detail, the sum of the Hall's bronze plaques and the natural light introduced from above give visitors a sense that this is a special place. Previously hidden at the heart of the museum (making its discovery almost an accident), it can now be viewed through glass at the front entrance lobby and entered as the climax of a full museum tour. Individual visits may differ, but the totality of experience is more important than any encounter with specific exhibition elements. Such details may vary, but the route of discovery is now always clear.

Main Street, Cooperstown, New York

The Glimmerglass Opera is an important part of the puzzle of Cooperstown. The opera is seasonal; it has a fairly short season. People come to Cooperstown to see the opera, but it attracts a very different crowd. Cooperstown is very family oriented—you take your kids to the Farmers' Museum. The Fenimore Art Museum is a little more serious.

MF: What are you most interested in? Baseball or Fenimore?

JFC: I would say both equally. Because I love art, and my grandfather founded both. He was primarily an art collector, but he loved the art of baseball, and I'm a little bit the way he was. I can't tell you this morning what the Chicago Cubs finished the season with. I can't tell you pitching stats from San Francisco. Do I wake up every morning dying to see baseball scores? No. But I love the game and the art of the game and the sport of the game and the history of the game.

We are more than a museum in that we have sixty-five living Hall of Fame members who are a very important part of what we do. I'm just crazy about being with the Hall of Fame members and trying to make their museum— their Hall of Fame—their honor, and be special to them.

The staff and I agreed we needed to have a renovation. The Hall of Fame had been added onto and renovated seventeen times since it opened in 1939, and it was very piecemeal work. The exhibition spaces needed to be reworked, opened up so that we got the proper flow through all floors of the museum and the library building and the connecting wing. It really now offers the visitor a great experience, and the visitors love our new layout and what it's allowed our curatorial staff to do in the galleries.

Top National Baseball Hall of Fame entrance lobby

Bottom Front facade

Contrast

"The juxtaposition of
old with new represents
historical continuity."

Brooklyn Academy of Music
Brooklyn, New York

Conversation
Harvey Lichtenstein
Former president
of the Brooklyn
Academy of Music

"Contrast" considers the Brooklyn
Academy of Music's facade restoration
and its radically new canopy, in which
glass is used as a structural element of
the design to form a grand, undulating
embellishment—an homage to both
Harvey Lichtenstein and Brooklyn.

Projects

Brooklyn Academy of Music
Brooklyn, New York, restoration in 1998

The new BAM was invented by Harvey
Lichtenstein. He took an all-but-abandoned
city-owned theater facility and created a
place where adventuresome New Yorkers
could discover the latest performing artists
and their often-controversial presentations.
The opera house of this multitheater center,
built in 1908, was Brooklyn's grandest
performing-arts complex and the first
such multiple-performance-hall building
in America. However, by 1967, when
Lichtenstein arrived, it had fallen on hard
times along with its derelict surrounding
neighborhood and was perceived as unsafe.
Today, BAM's success has stabilized
the neighborhood and spawned its own
cultural district, supported by New York City
government and an active, young audience.
Its Next Wave Festival brings performers
here from around the world to entertain a
public that gathers from all over the city.

The BAM Cultural District is now an officially
designated, multiblock area developed
by New York City. Lichtenstein imagined
a cultural district that would offer the
newest ideas in the visual and performing
arts and also stimulate creative activities
within Brooklyn itself. It was conceived as a
combination of existing nineteenth-century
buildings and entirely new structures, with
parks and redesigned streets intended to
establish a new residential community. Here
a mixture of artists' housing, rehearsal
and performance studios, galleries, and
offices are to be located in appropriately
diverse architecture costing less to achieve
than similar spaces in Manhattan.

The center of the district, BAM's 104-year-
old opera house, is a proud example of
beaux-arts design. The city originally
contracted with Lichtenstein to operate it
because no profitable use for its many large

spaces could be imagined. The second-floor ballroom had been converted to five classrooms by the Board of Education, and occasionally ill-attended music concerts took place in the dingy opera hall. Other areas of the building remained completely unused. What architectural premise could possibly bring this delapidated building back to life?

Restoration solely for traditional vocal and instrumental music was not feasible at that time. Instead, many different interventions have taken place. Under Lichtenstein's initiative, public, performing, and administrative spaces were repurposed to serve a variety of functions unimaginable in 1908. Although the original character of the opera house remains, the BAM Café (once a ballroom, transformed into a venue for live jazz and video presentations) and a four-screen multiplex (originally a recital hall) offer a variety of almost round-the-clock experiences. These popular programs appeal to a wide community audience.

While some interior architectural changes complement the original design, a new exterior glass canopy stands in deliberate contrast to the original building. It was certainly appropriate to restore the building's elegant, colorful facade to its original splendor. But to honor Harvey Lichtenstein's progressive spirit, it was obvious to me that a zestful, contemporary design was called for to contrast with Herts & Tallant's original design. This juxtaposition of old with new represents the historical continuity of BAM's nineteenth-century origins and Lichtenstein's twenty-first century vision for the arts. The result retains the rhythm of Herts & Tallant's great, decorative facade but uses glass in a way that is possible only now.

Brooklyn Academy of Music
Brooklyn, New York

The Brooklyn Academy of Music's opera house was originally designed in 1908 by Herts & Tallant, New York's premier theater architects, but by the 1960s their resplendent structure had been badly abused. In fear that it was structurally unsound, a fifteen-foot-tall rooftop cornice had been removed in the 1950s, together with five original three-story glass windows and decorative frames that had harmonized the beaux-arts composition. An unidentified designer had cluttered the center of the facade with a heavy and dark cast-iron canopy. Above this, the five great window spaces were filled with aluminum mullions composed of fat, incongruous horizontal stripes. This shorn and battered composition was a great embarrassment to Brooklyn. Worse still, water had penetrated the masonry walls, causing instability and some ominous bulges, and the entire remaining masonry facade clearly needed reconstruction. With audiences increasing, the front steps had been commandeered as informal lobby space, requiring a new and better canopy and a more festive appearance in general.

When first unveiled more than one hundred years ago, the facade's bold use of glazed color with terra-cotta ornament was the subject of much professional commentary; it continues to give a celebratory appearance to this great public monument. Since documentation was available that showed how the original cornice and decorative detail were installed, accurate replication could be achieved. By matching the original materials and colors, we could restore the building's sculptural profiles so that they could again meet the sky with authority. (We had already replaced the ugly horizontal aluminum 1950s window sashes with replicas of the original steel mullions).

The terra-cotta-faced bricks of the facade were removed to repair rusting internal steel columns and then reinstalled. In addition, many of the *putti* set in rondels around the entrance had lost some of their fingers and the details of their musical instruments. To ensure appropriate reconstruction, the contractors held a competition to find a craftsman with the right touch to recreate these elements. The resulting mockups of children's fingers, demonstrating each

Harvey Lichtenstein
Former president of the
Brooklyn Academy of Music

MF: What brought
you to Brooklyn?

HL: I had no experience running a theater. They said, "Apply, apply, apply!" So I applied. I remember when Seth Faison, who was then the chairman of the search committee, offered me the job. And after they offered me the job, I called up a guy who was chairman of the board of the New York City Center, which included the Ballet and the New York City Opera. He was a lawyer by the name of Baum. Morton Baum. I called him, and I said, "Mr. Baum, I've just had an offer from the Brooklyn Academy of Music, I just wanted to tell you." And he said, "Thank you for telling me, but I have a piece of advice to give you." And I said, "What is that, Mr. Baum?" And he said, "Those of us who have been looking at the cultural situation in New York know about the Brooklyn Academy of Music. We really think nothing can be done there. So I just want to warn you that it's a hard job." And I said, "Mr. Baum, I want to thank you very much for telling me that, and I understand what you're telling me, but I gotta take the job. I gotta do it. I applied for it, and nobody else is offering me a theater to run. So I'm going to take it. I'm going to take my chances." He said, "OK."

candidate's skill in reproducing these missing pieces, filled the construction trailer. Final reconstruction was accurate in both spirit and execution, having become an unexpected labor of love.

The top fifteen feet of cornice, balustrade, and cartouche were replaced with contemporary terra-cotta and colored-concrete reproductions, using the profiles and color scheme recorded in the original documentation. After damaged bricks of the facade were removed, some had to be recast with the same glazed terra-cotta finish as the original. Also included in restoration of the facade's original textured pattern was a cross-shaped unit featuring four lyres in honor of music. As always in masonry restoration, the most difficult color matching involved choosing a mortar that would seamlessly blend the new work with the old. It is remarkable how this exuberant facade continues to heighten anticipation of viewing a performance. Its design clearly marks this theater as a place outside everyday experience.

Oddly, the original facade had no pedestrian protection. Although Herts & Tallant had designed a fanciful cast-iron-and-glass canopy structure for their 1902 Lyceum Theater in Manhattan, they had provided nothing similar in Brooklyn. To offer a design that would imitate the original architects would be a foolish and needlessly sentimental pursuit, especially when viewed against the vitality of their existing work. What to do? A traditional cast-iron-and-glass structure would protect patrons and recall the early twentieth century but partially obscure the facade. I believed that views of the newly resplendent facade—especially when lit at night—should be part of the experience of stepping up into the building. To accomplish this, we used glass as a basic structural element of the canopy's construction, pushing the boundaries of its material strength. Contemporary technology offers a bold contrast between stainless-steel pipes and glass and the lavishly textured decorative wall behind. Sixty-five identical triangular glass panels undulate in a wavelike gesture that emphasizes the entrance doors and sheds water to the curb line below; this new, reflective expanse appears to partially float in front of the original facade. The canopy makes explicit a relationship between new and old, one that stimulates the discovery of both while honoring Harvey Lichtenstein's magnificent reinvention of BAM.

Top Opera house, 1925
Bottom Original canopy, 1980

<u>Above</u> Detail of restored terra cotta and the new canopy

<u>Right</u> Terra-cotta cherub

Time

"The assumption that restoration involves reproducing the original does not always apply. Interpreting the past is sometimes preferable to attempting to re-create it."

Brooklyn Academy of Music Harvey Theater Brooklyn, New York

Conversation
Harvey Lichtenstein
Former president
of the Brooklyn
Academy of Music

Radio City Music Hall New York, New York

Conversation
Kent Barwick
Former president of the
Municipal Art Society of
New York and former chair of
the New York City Landmarks
Preservation Commission

The sixth theme is "Time." Here, two theaters are contrasted: the Brooklyn Academy of Music's Harvey and Radio City Music Hall. These buildings embody widely divergent views about the aims of restoration.

Projects

Brooklyn Academy of Music Harvey Theater
Brooklyn, New York, restoration in 1987

Radio City Music Hall
New York, New York, restoration in 1999

The assumption that restoration involves reproducing the original does not always apply. As other projects in this book have illustrated, interpreting the past is sometimes preferable to attempting to re-create it, which is often impossible. The following two projects express perfectly valid but totally different ideas about the presence of time in restoration.

The Harvey was a genuine ruin created by water damage over years of neglect and eventual abandonment. Our aim in this project was not to return to a specific point in time but rather to display the passage of time. Built as the Majestic in 1904, its history permitted nature to create its own environment, which Harvey Lichtenstein ultimately reclaimed as a theatrical setting for director Peter Brook, who kept evidence of decay intact.

In contrast, the refurbished Radio City Music Hall was intended to look new. Indeed, when it opened in 1932, it was the snazziest, newest thing in New York City. Nothing could compare with its breathtaking public spaces, whose innovative design eschewed traditional plaster ornament and illuminated wall sconces in favor of surfaces that glowed with reflected light and decorative textile patterns bearing motifs from contemporary entertainment. Although world renowned for its stage spectacles, by 1978 it had been threatened with demolition. But despite wear and tear over more than sixty years, in 1996 both New York City and State rallied with Tishman Speyer and the Madison Square Garden Company to completely restore all its public spaces, unveiling an interior that was once again polished and new. It now denies its age, as absolutely every surface gleams with the fresh promise of an earlier era's faith in the future.

Both these projects were created with
an awareness of time. We celebrated
it by embracing the Harvey ever-changing
history; Radio City was restored to its
original appearance in defiance of time.
The effort to make Radio City again dazzle
and generate profit went beyond mere
re-creation of materials, paints, finishes,
and textile designs. It brought this legendary
venue up to contemporary standards
of illumination with a shimmer of reflected
light that once again is unequaled in
its emotional impact. By contrast, the
Harvey's commitment to new ideas and
nonprofit status permitted a more inclusive
approach to restoration. Although initially
condemned as a display of "radical
chic," the Harvey has seen its reputation
rise as judgment has mellowed and
audiences have grown accustomed to its
no-nonsense, evocative interior, which
exhibits a pleasing warmth and intimacy
not found in traditional restoration projects.
However different, neither approach
to restoration negates the other.

Brooklyn Academy of Music
Harvey Theater
Brooklyn, New York

Although BAM now celebrates 150 years of performance activity, America's oldest performing-arts center had suffered a great decline in the 1960s, as its Brooklyn audiences had aged and moved to the suburbs and its neighborhood had become unsafe. Meanwhile, with few exceptions, live performance on a declining Broadway had become dull and formulaic.

Harvey Lichtenstein's decision to take charge of BAM changed both the institution and its borough, creating a theater with a reputation for presenting new ideas and talents that often originated across the sea. New Yorkers were surprised by new concepts of staging and abstract explorations in many media, all of which were presented with great vigor. This created a must-see environment for those in the know. In the process, BAM's shabby conditions gradually were improved so that audiences, performers, and technical crews no longer suffered the many indignities once brought about by its decaying physical plant.

As part of his project of bringing exceptional work to BAM, Lichtenstein wanted to present Peter Brook's production of *The Mahabharata*, a nine-hour epic comparable only to the Old Testament in its ambition. Brook agreed to come to Brooklyn if Lichtenstein could find him an appropriate theater. One block from the opera house, the Majestic theater was discovered moldering away; Lichtenstein then pulled off the almost-magical, only-in-Brooklyn feat of presenting a nine-hour nonprofit production for a limited run and securing money from the city to restore the theater.

Having performed *The Mahabharata* around the world, Brook felt at home in the environment of this ruined theater where nature had created its own character. His idea was to present the great Indian legend in a setting such as one might find in nature, embracing the ruined condition of the eighty-year-old theater. In Paris, he had staged performances in a run-down music hall, Les Bouffes du Nord (located by the Gare du Nord railroad station), to achieve a similar startling effect. Appreciating the character of surfaces damaged by water, careless use, and indifference, Brook lauded this environment that exhibited the assaults of time.

Harvey Lichtenstein
Former president of the
Brooklyn Academy of Music

HL: We needed a theater to do *The Mahabharata*, which Peter Brook had done in France at the theater Les Bouffes du Nord in Paris. He wanted a theater, but he didn't want any of the theaters we had. So he saw this space, and he said, "Let's see if we can do it," and I gave it some character like the one he has in Paris, which is also an old theater that he reclaimed and remodeled.

MF: What gave you the idea to make it look like it was really in bad shape?

HL: That was Peter Brook's idea. He wanted people to know it was an old theater that was replanned. So it had some history, and the history would be shown.

Pierre Boulez came with his orchestra and played a concert there. And I asked about the acoustics, and he said, "The acoustics are fine, Harvey—don't worry about it."

After we finished and Peter was rehearsing in the theater, a friend of mine—Teresa Stratas, who was a soprano at the Met—wanted to come and see it. So I said, "Come on, Teresa, I'll take you there." And I took her there, and we sat in what had been a box at the top of what is now the orchestra while Peter was rehearsing. And she looked at

Such a premise was completely unheard of in New York, where restoration was long assumed to mean returning a building to a simulation of its original appearance as closely as physically possible. Indeed, early audiences at the Harvey were nervous, finding the theater unfinished instead of evocative. But those who understood that performances of *The Mahabharata* inevitably involve the passage of time greatly enjoyed witnessing the epic in an interior where nature's powerful and random transformation of structure, plaster, and paint were clearly visible.

Far Left Majestic theater, original facade, 1980s

Left Majestic theater under reconstruction, 1986

Above Harvey theater, restored facade

Brook liked neither the frontal proscenium configuration of the original theater nor its nine-hundred-seat capacity. By raising the stage one story, we were able to bring the playing area forward in front of the proscenium, continuing the rake of the mezzanine seating to meet the stage. A seating bowl was thus created, similar to that of the Bouffes du Nord. At Brook's request, technical director Jean-Guy Lecat (a longtime collaborator) joined us as we considered how to reconfigure seating levels in relation to the new stage height. The resulting seven-hundred-seat arrangement provides a great degree of intimacy, bringing audience and performers together in the same space. To give audiences in the upper-balcony level clear views of this new stage position, the balcony's front five rows were removed and barstool seating was installed to permit steep sightlines. These seats are prized by the young—not for comfort, but for being cheap and offering an unusual vantage point.

Displaying rough finishes left by plaster removal, a variety of wall colors revealing various layers of use, and steel fireproofing, the interior was raw. To ensure these surroundings would not distract from performances, Brook's scenic artist Chloe

it, and she said, "Harvey, when is it going to be finished?" And I said, "Teresa, it's finished. This is what it is. This is finished. This is it." And she looked at me, and she said, "Harvey, I was just going to tell you: Why don't you leave it like this?"

It's a beautiful theater. Everyone who goes there loves playing in it. William Christie, the conductor of Jean-Baptiste Lully's *Atys*, played the concert Sunday night. I went to see him afterward, and he said, "This is a wonderful theater. I know how it was made for *The Mahabharata*, and I love it. The sound is wonderful. The connection with the audience is great." The people who play there love it. The actors love it. I'm so proud to have that theater there. With the Majestic theater, if you saw it, and saw the shape it was in, you wouldn't believe it—it was really an absolute mess. The water was flowing in. There was water all over the floor. Seats were falling apart. It was a bloody mess—to reclaim it was a miracle.

MF: What was BAM's reaction when you told them that you wanted to turn that into a theater? Did they think you were crazy?

Obolensky softened some contrasts and introduced others, adding mirrors in the lobby to make the whole appear more unified—a subtle process that reinforced the building's derelict character.

The result has proven to be remarkably flexible. Without any basic changes to the fixed mezzanine seating, the forward stage area can be configured for either audience or performers by using loose chairs. An orchestra pit can be created in front of the proscenium frame, and a house curtain can be used to separate backstage from the auditorium for traditional presentations. Alternately, the full expanse of the stage can be open so that performances occupy the entire space, with lighting indicating playing areas.

Although our work met every building-code requirement for public safety, we could not get a building permit because the auditorium looked so unfinished. Building-code officials said, "It just doesn't look right." However, maintaining that aesthetics were the province of the architect, we compromised by agreeing that I would sign and stamp an official document certifying that the requirements of code had been observed and that the aesthetics were professionally acceptable. Armed with this paperwork, the Department of Buildings issued the needed Certificate of Occupancy.

In describing the results to the public, we call this a restoration—not a re-creation of the past but rather a restoration of use. Dedicated in honor of Harvey Lichtenstein in 1999, it is beloved by performers for its rough-and-ready interior and intimate seating configuration; its flexibility continues to accommodate such an amazing range of productions that audiences can depend on discovering something new with each visit.

HL: We needed money. We figured we needed about four-and-a half million, but actually it cost us about five-and-a-half. But we went to the city, and we couldn't get an answer. I remember I was in Europe going to some festivals with my wife the summer before. I got a call in the south of France from the mayor's office, here in New York. And they said, "Harvey, we've got four-and-a-half million dollars for you, for redoing the Majestic theater." And I said, "Thank you." And they said that the city owned the theater, because nobody paid taxes on it. So they took over the theater and boarded it up.

Harvey theater, orchestra

Radio City Music Hall
New York, New York

The story of Rockefeller Center is one of triumph: staggering profit, critical acclaim, and public affection. However, the project was initially castigated by critics such as Lewis Mumford, who denounced it in the March 1931 *New Republic* with salvos like: "If this is the best our architects can do with freedom, they deserve to remain in chains."

Such vituperation was equaled only by the opening night of Radio City Music Hall in 1932—an even more abject failure. Walter Lippmann proclaimed in the *New York Herald Tribune* that Radio City was like "a great pedestal [built] to sustain a peanut."* The hall was magnificent, but performers appeared diminished in size, reduced to ciphers against the giant curves of the hall, the width of a city block. Today we have astonishing levels of amplification, projections, and video or LED images to enhance live performances. Even so, the flamboyant stagings of circuses or rock bands (or at the least, a Tony Bennett or a Bette Midler, with the help of much technological enhancement) are required to fully engage audiences at Radio City.

This story began in 1928, when John D. Rockefeller, Jr., acquired a large plot of land half a mile south of Central Park. Concerned about protecting family properties on East Fifty-Third and Fifty-Fourth Streets from development, he became part of a syndicate proposing to build a new Metropolitan Opera House between Forty-Eighth and Forty-Ninth Streets. The land was owned by Columbia University, and the project was to be called Metropolitan Square. An opera house would be the centerpiece of the composition, flanked by two office buildings intended to provide subsidy for the opera.

From this modest beginning, Rockefeller Center's creation became a complex tale involving numerous collaborators. It drew on the talents of eight architects and designers under the guiding spirit of Rockefeller, who envisioned a new urban center where business offices, retail stores, and entertainment would all come together to pursue profit in a planned environment.

---

*See Daniel Okrent, *Great Fortune: The Epic of Rockefeller Center* (New York: Penguin, 2004), 244.

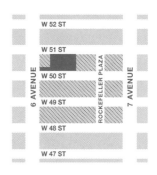

Kent Barwick
Former president of the Municipal Art Society of New York and former chair of the New York City Landmarks Preservation Commission

KB: Rockefeller Center announced in 1978 that after years of losing money, it was going to close Radio City Music Hall. The time for that kind of entertainment and that size of house had passed. There was a public outcry of dismay, and the Landmarks Commission calendared it for a hearing to consider making it an interior landmark.

As it happened, I was just coming in as the new chair of the Landmarks Commission, and my first real day on the job was going to be the hearing on Radio City Music Hall. In the week prior to this hearing, my predecessor, Beverly Moss Spatt, announced her view (which she later expressed in front of the whole commission) that the landmarks law was unconstitutional on its face as it applied to theaters. She had apparently come to this view after discussions with Alton Marshall. Al Marshall ran Rockefeller Center in those days—he was a very capable, powerful man who had worked for Nelson Rockefeller for years, including when Nelson Rockefeller was the governor. He was the governor's secretary, which is sort of the general head of staff. He was a smart

The development's emergence during the Great Depression served as an unintended testament of faith in the capitalist system. Rockefeller and his construction manager, John R. Todd, a hard-driving man placed in charge of scheduling and money, sought to prove to a skeptical America that the free-enterprise system could still produce results that were both civilized and profitable.

The 1929 Wall Street crash made the original idea of an elitist opera house sponsored by wealthy patrons impractical, and the entire project was reconceived. At the project's center, a corporate high-rise complex for General Electric, Radio Corporation of America (RCA), and Radio-Keith-Orpheum (RKO) was designed to be a powerhouse mass-entertainment complex, replacing the opera house. Other changes followed. Migrating from its original Fifth Avenue site to Sixth Avenue, the performance hall eventually morphed into Radio City, a six-thousand-seat hall for popular entertainment.

Clearly, the strength of Radio City's design is a result of the give-and-take of a lengthy collaborative process. Of the team of eight architects who defined the Rockefeller Center project, Raymond Hood was the greatest design talent. Formative ideas also came from those who had worked on earlier schemes at the same site for Metropolitan Square. For Radio City's main performance space, the Music Hall, Donald Deskey contributed some interiors (and a carpet with a design called "Singing Women"), working with eight other artists, including Stuart Davis. Professor Stanley McCandless of Yale designed a four-color lighting system whose cove lights washed over the ceiling layers with either gradual overall color changes or a parade of different hues. Ruth Reeves upholstered the rear and outside walls in a dazzling pattern that repeated diagonally and cleverly represented multiple forms of popular entertainment.

Of all the unusual relationships formed in the construction of the center, none is more startling than that of Rockefeller and impresario Samuel L. "Roxy" Rothafel. "Junior" was taciturn, withdrawn, and conservative; Roxy was all showbiz, a man of exceptional brilliance and unequaled salesmanship. These two mismatched titans were brought together by commercial considerations; transformation of the Metropolitan Opera House into the populist palace of Radio City brought about the pressure to make a profit. Rothafel's previous commercial success made him an invaluable part of this real-

lawyer and a powerful person and obviously a representative of a very powerful family, and so he persuaded Mrs. Spatt, who chose the morning of this public hearing to make this announcement. I hadn't met any of the other commissioners. An hour before the public hearing, there was a coffee set up at City Hall for me to meet the other commissioners and for them to meet the new chairman, and it was there that Mrs. Spatt announced her opposition. Then she went into the Board of Estimate's chamber, where the hearing was going to be held, and shifted around the place cards. She didn't like where she was sitting.

She was a very bright woman who had been trained as a planner. She was a member, back in the Mayor John Lindsay years, of the city Planning Commission and always in the opposition—not necessarily wrongly, but often in opposition to things that Lindsay and Donald Elliott, who was head of the Planning Commission, wanted to do. She finally lost her post as a member of the Planning Commission, but when Abraham Beame came in, he appointed Beverly to be the head of the Landmarks Commission. What she did was to bring the Landmarks Commission into a much more constructive role in terms of its relationship to planning and community development, and she did quite a number of very

estate gamble, despite differences in personal taste. (Who would have imagined the conservative John D. sponsoring publicity photos of the long, bare legs of the Rockettes?) Roxy's genius for creating large-scale moneymaking entertainment seemed to guarantee Radio City's profitability. Although lost to us, exchanges between these dissimilar talents must have formed a truly rare collision of cultures.

good things, but I don't think this was necessarily one of them.

As it happened, I had been involved a few years prior to that time in drafting the law relating to interior landmarks. It was based on a well-established principle in the public accommodations section of the Civil Rights Act, which established

Opposite Radio City Music Hall auditorium

Left Choral balconies

Above Auditorium under restoration

Rothafel specifically oversaw the hall's design. He was the consummate showman of that time, and his vision established the theater's configuration, operation, and presentation form. Some say he should be given credit for the great, glowing arches that define the auditorium, although there was precedent for this design in Benjamin Morris's original scheme for the Metropolitan Opera. Rothafel claimed the idea came to him while watching a sunset at sea. He also insisted that unlike other movie palaces with their giant balconies, Radio City should have three short balconies at the rear of the hall so that everyone in the audience would be given a matchless view of the entire auditorium. This permits even the last rows of each seating section to experience the radiating curves of the enormous space.

One legacy of the original Radio City is radical in its simplicity: placement of a light-filled screen continuously radiating over both walls and ceiling, making no distinction between the two. Prior to its construction, every theater in the world was designed with a ceiling that was placed on top of its walls, much like putting the top on a pot. In one heroic gesture of concentric, fluted curves, all the various surfaces of Radio City's vast hall became one.

that places that were customarily open to the public (which included restaurants, train stations, hotels, and theaters) were subject to public regulation. When it came up in the Civil Rights Act, people in the South decided that their restaurants were private and their hotels were private, and they had the right to exclude blacks. And the Supreme Court found otherwise.

This was already pretty well established by the time we were working on the amendments to the landmarks law, which was at the end of the Lindsay administration, before Beame had come in. And so, while there were many people in the real-estate industry who probably thought it was socialist or communist or whatnot to deal with interiors, the federal courts had already dealt with it in the context of civil rights. So I wasn't initially persuaded by Mrs. Spatt or by Al Marshall, who came in and met me privately and announced the same views. He announced that he had been one of the authors of the original landmarks law, which he apparently had never had

Movies made actors appear larger than life-size, and they could have dominated this great interior, but Rothafel's dream for opening night was a perverse novelty: he insisted on banishing movies in favor of the older vaudeville format. Stage productions at that time were struggling to compete with movies, which were advancing into sound and featured such spectacles as train wrecks, hurricanes, and biblical pageantry. Radio City's first performance, presented with great panache by Rothafel, was a four-and-a-half-hour failure. His attempt to revive vaudeville with a high-class review format including performances by Martha Graham, Ray Bolger, and the Flying Wallendas, among others, was a profound mistake that left audiences bewildered. The scale of this giant room dwarfed performers, and even Martha Graham's troupe was criticized for looking like mice running around the fifty-foot-diameter turntable.

sufficient credit for. He knew a lot about the law—he was a very good lawyer—and he felt that it was very inappropriate to include an interior. I then consulted with some of the leading lawyers in New York and got a different view.

Very important, long discussions continued over whether Radio City Music Hall should be a landmark. The first meeting at City Hall, every single seat was filled. There were obviously groups like the Municipal Art Society and others that were lobbying very hard, and they weren't just lobbying by testifying. They had gotten the Rockettes to come down and dance on the steps of City Hall. So there was a lot of public activity pushing the matter forward. And it obviously

Left Panther mural in women's lounge
Right "Singing Women" auditorium carpet, Donald Deskey

As a result, Radio City's entertainment formula was changed to the ideal family combination of movies and a stage show, matching that of Rothafel's former showplace, the Roxy, located a block to the west. Rothafel was fired shortly after the opening; the only surviving trace of his vision was Russell Markert's use of his former dance troupe the Roxyettes for the Music Hall's Christmas show. Reborn as the Rockettes, their precision tap dancing continues to delight audiences to this day.

With the advent of larger and more ambitious talking movies, the movie-plus-show format was in turn gradually phased out across America in favor of movies alone. But by the 1970s, Hollywood's preoccupation with sex and violence produced movies ill-suited for family fare. And with a public accustomed to the type of glitzy spectacle presented in Las Vegas, Radio City's stage shows, with their flapping painted scenery, began to seem hopelessly dated.

was not only a significant piece of architecture but something very significant in the cultural life of the city and certainly warranted consideration as a landmark that deserved to be protected. In the meantime, Mr. Marshall promised that if we designated the building, they would sue, and that they would likely not only succeed but overturn the law. He instead offered to enter into an agreement where we wouldn't tear it down without some further discussion. And that was an offer that had to be dealt with seriously.

This was all going on in winter 1977–1978. I didn't come in with the wave of commissioners,

This once-proud quintessential New York showplace had outlived its entertainment formula. The orchestra, glee club, and ballet company were no more. Even the Christmas show could not keep the place alive year-round. In 1978, plans to close Radio City were announced. Compromise was instead struck, with a new producing organization created by the state's Urban Development Corporation in the vain hope that a revitalized hall could again find audiences with a version of its original presentation formula.

By 1996, real-estate developers Tishman Speyer took control of Rockefeller Center and were casting about for new ideas and talents to re-create Radio City as an entertainment destination. Surely, they thought, a six-thousand-seat house in New York City could find its audience if properly marketed. As the result of a competition, it was leased to the Madison Square Garden Company, a corporation sponsoring all forms of live entertainment. This conglomerate planned to broadcast videos "live from Radio City," drawing on the theater's history of popular spectacle as a branding device. In the Garden's media empire, the hall would be promoted like Las Vegas, with the Rockettes and the Christmas Spectacular forming a major component of its allure. As a result, Madison Square Garden paid for a first-rate restoration.

With the exception of the marble wainscoting and lobby mirrors silvered in gold, every surface in the public spaces of Radio City has been restored as new. The vestibule's black-and-red runners, its gilded ceiling's indirect light fixtures, and the refinished bronze of the ticket booths gleam again. Ezra Winter's glowing mural has been restored to the grand foyer, along with draperies that extend the entire height of the four-story space. The balcony fascia—once painted dark brown—and the newly reflective ceiling have been regilded. Most important, Donald Deskey's original carpet design has been reinstalled with its full twelve-panel pattern of musical-instrument abstractions set in a grid of contrasting warm tones.

The lower lobby again features its original diagonal carpet pattern, joining the diamond-shaped mirrored columns that once guided visitors in from the Sixth Avenue subway. Murals have been restored throughout, and lozenge-shaped lighting fixtures have new downlight illumination tucked in their radiating fins. This lobby's lounges and restrooms have had their original finishes restored, with furniture and carpeting based on period photographs and the Deskey Archive

because my predecessor would not relinquish her post. (She wouldn't give back the car, either.) She was a very difficult person, but she did so many great things that you forgave her. And again, this offer from such a prominent family, with so much at stake, was something that was reviewed and discussed.

The only thing the commission could do—which it did—was go ahead and designate the property.

But there was something else going on that was significant here. There was a lieutenant governor in New York State from 1975 to 1978 named Mary Anne Krupsak. She was lieutenant governor to Hugh Carey (he didn't get along with her particularly), and she asked the Urban Development Corporation (UDC) to step in. Richard Kahn was head of the UDC, and the UDC came in and took over the management of Radio City Music Hall and began to program the hall. They became very engaged in demonstrating that Radio City Music Hall could in fact survive.

The future of Radio City Music Hall had been the subject of all kinds of stories in the newspaper, and, as I said, the Rockettes decided to weigh in against their employers to fight for the music hall. They realized that if the music hall disappeared, then they would too. So it was something that the public was very focused on for at least six months, and during that period of time, it started to make money.

For all the years that Radio City Music Hall had been written about and revered, with groups like the Art Deco Society giving tours and oohing and aahing over it, I don't think a lot of money had been put into it, so it had become very run-down. Some of the furniture had been removed. Nelson Rockefeller had taken one of the paintings out and given it to the Museum of Modern Art. Nobody had reinvested in it in a long, long time.

The Rockettes are showgirls who are highly disciplined, and for them to stand up and go public and fight for Radio City Music Hall was a smart thing to do (because otherwise they would have lost their jobs), but it took a lot of courage to

at the Smithsonian Cooper-Hewitt, National Design Museum. The Stuart Davis mural *Men Without Women* has been returned from the Museum of Modern Art for the men's lounge, and the women's lounge features a refreshed mural detailing the history of cosmetics. Numerous historic sources were consulted in restoring the six individual upstairs lounges and restrooms.

The great hall's ceiling has been completely resurfaced with a sprayed stipple finish similar to the hand-applied original. Lighting coves have been reset with illumination almost double the original intensity but still using red, blue, green, and amber glass filters. Seats have been replaced by their original manufacturer, once again upholstered in russet mohair with black piping, and the walls are resplendent in Ruth Reeves's incomparable fabric, made sound-transparent for acoustic absorption. The great house curtain was woven in Queens by Scalamandre and is so large it had to be transported in three sections and sewn together onstage. It is still operated by original eighty-year-old machinery.

Radio City was conceived as a great palace for everyone, built to make money in the hope of better times to come. It was a showcase for all new forms of design and a testament of faith in America's future. Although often referred to as "art deco" (after the decorative style introduced at the 1925 Paris Exposition), the designs of Rockefeller Center and Radio City are much more abstract and simplified than the original French decorative style. I prefer to call Rockefeller Center "American modernism" after its American roots and forward-looking optimism. Therefore, unlike restorations intended to emphasize a project's feeling of antiquity, the restored Radio City is intended to dazzle audiences just as it did when new, not only reproducing original surfaces and finishes but, most important, increasing the level of indirect lighting to match contemporary expectations for illumination.

The Music Hall's current moneymaker is the Christmas Spectacular, but who knows how long this adapted vaudeville format will survive? What would happen if new, younger talents were given an opportunity to present performances? It may be that the hall's large size will ultimately defeat efforts to find new audiences. Or it may be that future modes of electronic presentation will give birth to new ideas of spectacle, allowing Radio City to transcend the nostalgic allure of its past glory and find new audiences.

do that. And they haven't forgotten. When I was leaving the Municipal Art Society in 2008, there was a nice party given for me in a tent in front of the Seagram Building. You know, one of the events where they hand over medals and gold watches and say nice things. The culmination of it was that the Rockettes showed up and danced! Someone remembered that they owed the Municipal Art Society—not that they owed me anything, but I think they were glad that I did what I did at the time.

Top Ladies' lounge, detail
Bottom Rockette with businessmen

Public Space

"Each project benefits from the everyday delights of common experience, so that members of the public become citizen-performers in a theater of community."

Ridge Hill
Yonkers, New York

Conversation

Bruce Ratner
Executive vice president of Forest City Enterprises, Inc., and chair and CEO of Forest City Ratner Companies

Bryant Park
New York, New York

Conversations

Marian Heiskell
Chair of the New 42nd Street board of directors

Daniel Biederman
President of the Bryant Park Restoration Corporation

Lynden Miller
Designer of restored Bryant Park gardens

United States
Federal Courthouse
Jackson, Mississippi

Conversations

Les Shepherd
Chief architect for the General Services Administration

Joseph Valerio
Peer reviewer on the General Services Administration's Design Excellence Program selection committee

William H. Barbour, Jr.
Senior judge for the Southern District of Mississippi

Fletcher Cox
Artist, designer, and fabricator of courtroom doors

Katy Stone
Artist for courthouse entrance-ramp metalwork

Projects

Ridge Hill
Yonkers, New York, 2012

Bryant Park
New York, New York, restoration in 1995

United States Federal Courthouse
Jackson, Mississippi, 2010

"Public Space" contrasts the design approaches of three different projects: one in the suburbs of New York City; one within the city; and one in Jackson, Mississippi, showing how each responds differently to its community.

Each time an audience gathers for a theatrical performance, a new, evanescent community is formed. The creators of these diverse assemblages vary in their level of experience and knowledge, but each performance brings strangers together to share the ritual of live presentation. The results can be ephemeral or become permanently lodged in memory, but their experience is a public act of participation.

It is not surprising (given my affection for theater) that so much of the work I represent in this book has been created for public buildings, or that it has been enhanced by a direct concern for how people feel and look in the places we have made for them.

Until recently, New York City's public spaces were most often developed by government rather than by private entities, although some great outdoor rooms have been built by private educational institutions. Commercial gathering places were sustained by public streets, while parks provided recreation and relaxation.

Our streets remain a constant source of public activity and impromptu encounter. Recently, with the advent of corporate sponsorship, the private sector has entered into development of public space.

For the most part, early attempts at profit-making public attractions were financial failures until Rockefeller Center opened its first buildings in 1932. This project, enthusiastically promoted as "a city within a city," created a carefully planned, programmed, and maintained domain whose public spaces created a new urban focus. It gave New York City a new midtown, and remains open to the public without charge, sponsoring botanical displays and seasonal activities.

But, of course, it is not a true city, because no one has ever lived there.

It is instructive to see how a range of contemporary communities and institutions develop public space. Private developers approach the stewardship of public spaces in terms of how they can best increase profitability. Parks are the original public spaces of American cities, and their public amenities typically have been funded through taxes. Until recently, maintaining New York City's public space was solely the responsibility of the city, but that is changing as the creation of Business Improvement Districts has become a popular strategy for enhancing neighborhood business environments. The federal government can create major additions to the public realm through construction of institutional projects—for example, courthouses, those important symbols of the legal process. But alas, these civic spaces are also increasingly subject to required security control to limit their public access.

Ridge Hill, a shopping destination configured like a traditional Westchester town, was created all at once by a private real-estate company, Forest City Ratner. It is an eighty-acre retail development situated in Yonkers between two high-speed roadways: the New York State Thruway and the Sprain Brook Parkway, both major access routes to New York City. Its public spaces are controlled and maintained by Forest City, sustained by income from 1.5 million square feet of surrounding retail and entertainment facilities. This instant community was informed by the varied character of small towns in Westchester. Admission to all public areas is free, and people can assemble as they choose, participating in programmed activities, shopping, or just enjoying a schmooze. Its central square offers seasonal activities for both adults and children. Instead of the deadening culture and fixed environment of the indoor shopping mall, the center offers pedestrians possibilities for the casual and unpredictable interactions found in village life.

Our new architecture for Bryant Park strives for a different type of authenticity, borrowing elements from traditional park design. Trelliswork, pergolas, ines, and flowers are all used to create an extension of the park landscape rather than a stand-alone piece of architecture. My hope is that sitting inside its restaurant conveys the feeling of being within the park. This structure is intended to complement the New York Public Library's great rear wall of white marble and to surround its book stacks with an extension of the park's landscape.

Our 413,000-square-foot courthouse in Jackson, Mississippi, creates a new public center for this capital city. Jackson's exuberant beaux-arts capitol building is set on a hill eight blocks to the north. We configured the courthouse's six-story volumes around a central rotunda, establishing a major axis with the capitol and giving a new definition to the city's downtown.

Each of these three projects shapes its public space to make visitors feel welcome and to encourage participation in the public realm. None employs imagery intended to express authoritarian control or political power. Each benefits from the everyday delights of common experience, so that members of the public become citizen-performers in a theater of community. Although the clients' roles in sponsoring these activities vary, each of these institutions must enjoy public support for continued success. The diversity found here is the measure of each project's intent and long-term survival.

Ridge Hill
Yonkers, New York

A desire in each community for access to retail amenities, civic services, transportation, and entertainment determined the form of traditional Westchester towns and public spaces. Each has its own character—a direct response to site geography, local custom, and economic factors. Because these places grew over time, they possess an authenticity that is impossible to replicate. By contrast, development projects like Ridge Hill, created solely as retail centers, must be built all at once. Although responsive to change and the mobile fortunes of retail activities, these places must instantly create a sense of permanence that authentic villages achieve only through the layering of time.

A number of retail pseudo-villages and outlet malls have been built in America—most notably the first, Country Club Plaza in Kansas City, Missouri. In 1924 it was designed to masquerade as an authentic town with a Spanish character, featuring decorated stucco walls and tile roofs not naturally occurring in the Midwest. But despite its obvious lack of architectural authenticity, Country Club Plaza has become one of the top sixty retail public spaces in the world.

In contrast, Ridge Hill uses an original design language of bold patterning and three-dimensional display formed from layers of different materials. It does not attempt to replicate indigenous buildings. Unlike an enclosed mall, the project features open streets, a central square, pedestrian bridges with roofs, and walkways and garden landscaping, all available to the public. Stylistic variety exists, but facades of different buildings relate to a common vocabulary (with a few odd fellows thrown in). It will be considerably altered over the years as tenants join and depart from the project, but the first phase of Ridge Hill defines a design whose authority is strong enough to be maintained through the inevitable changes that occur on any retail street in America.

Organization of the tenant mix and location of individual stores and entertainment facilities at

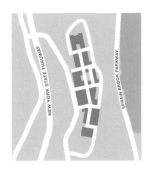

Bruce Ratner
Executive vice president of Forest City Enterprises, Inc., and chair and CEO of Forest City Ratner Companies

BR: Ridge Hill is a lifestyle center. It's got a lot of restaurants; it's got very few big boxes; it's got a department store, Lord and Taylor; it's got a lot of large-name category stores (like Marshall's), but it's basically small stores and restaurants.

I've never seen a mall well made. So I wanted to do something different, and I wanted to use Hugh. Management fought me on it. They did not want to use a design architect to do something he had never done before—a mall. That was a pretty risky thing from their point of view. Did he know how to do it?

We prevailed; Hugh it was. And Hugh did a design. We walked the site a number of times, and there were a lot of nice trees on it. Hugh had to work with an existing layout. (It would have been a lot of work to get to a point of knowledge where you would know how to lay out a lifestyle center. I think he easily could have done it, but it would have taken him a lot of homework to get up to speed.)

It was already supposed to be like a town center—that was a given—but the question was: What should the architecture be? Should it be retro? Should

Ridge Hill are Forest City's responsibility, but the built environment was designed by H3 in collaboration with Studio 5 Partnership (construction documents), Oehme van Sweden (landscape architecture), Stantec (graphics), and Cline Bettridge Bernstein (lighting). Together we have made a place that has the intimacy and variety of Main Street America without copying its traditional formal vocabulary.

Patterned elevations feature compositions made in a series of layers using different designs and materials: brick, expanded metal, zinc shingles, and extruded metal panels. A variety of brick patterns recalls the early craftsman vocabulary of Westchester buildings, particularly those found in Scarsdale and Bronxville, or the Victorian structures of Yonkers. Although the brickwork in older buildings was laid by hand, Ridge Hill's walls are covered with one-inch-thick brick tile faces embedded into concrete panels built in Canadian shops and trucked down interstate highways to New York. These panels—some thirty feet long and ten feet high—can be installed quickly, and their hooked corner pieces successfully mimic solid brickwork.

Ridge Hill's plan is based on the typical density of a traditional American Main Street and offers both automobile and pedestrian routes. It is placed on top of a prominent rock outcropping, with a configuration of two- and three-story buildings joined by covered walkways and connected to six-story parking garages placed at the perimeter. Pedestrian access from the parking structures occurs at different elevations onto street level or upper walkways that feature retail spaces and many vantage points for people-watching. These structures define an open-air town center with remarkable views of the surrounding landscape. Additional amenities include flower gardens, interactive fountains, play sculpture, and benches. Present and future high-rise buildings will include rental housing.

Unlike enclosed malls with their stultifying uniformity, Ridge Hill surrounds the public with all of nature's variety, as the four seasons provide the continual stimulation of changing light and atmosphere. This ensures that no two encounters will be the same and return visits will offer the unexpected. Informal socializing—the delight of chance encounters and personal greetings among neighbors—creates a relaxed atmosphere for impulse buying. The central goal of this project is, once again, the creation of community.

it be like an old town center in Oberlin or Chagrin Falls, Ohio, or some other place like that? And I think the conclusion was: No. Retro is not really what we want to do, because it never really works. So the question is: What is Westchester?

Hugh had a lot of different pictures that he had taken, trying to look at the style. He came up with a style which I think really works. It's a style that has a jazz aspect and a lot of movement to it. And it's got articulation, and it's got color; it's got variety. It's good architecture.

We put art in our projects. In this case, I went to Tom Otterness; he'd done a jungle-gym before, so I went to him, and I said, "Tom, we don't have trillions of dollars to spend. Can you do this?" And he says, "Yup. We'll do it for you." So he did this jungle-gym for us, which is beautiful. It's right near the commons.

National Amusements is the theater operator; it's going to have a restaurant inside, so you can eat meals in there when you're watching a movie.

They also do something called SummerStage, which we run with the New York City Parks Foundation. That programming is in a lot of other parks now, too. What's nicer than free music in a park?

Top Site plan
Bottom Overall view: second level

Bryant Park
New York, New York

The design of Bryant Park, completed in 1934 under the supervision of Aymar Embury II, was one of Robert Moses's first park projects. In 1992 a newly restored park reopened with a new landscape design by Hanna/Olin Ltd. William Hollingsworth Whyte, Jr., who consulted closely on this latest revitalization, was the patron saint of Bryant Park's transformation. His belief in schmoozing as a profound component of public behavior greatly influenced reconfiguration of a space where people now gather to talk, find a place in the sun, or even just enjoy solitude.

Whyte's ideas led to loose seating (made available without charge throughout the park), allowing visitors to arrange themselves alone or in intimate groups and avoid the tyranny of fixed park benches. It was common wisdom that this radical idea could not work, because park seating had to be bolted down or it would be stolen. In practice, replacement seating more typically is required because of maintenance issues than theft.

Whyte also insisted the park's access to the street should be increased. He recommended two new street-level entrances, one each in the middle of the north and south perimeters. In addition, he suggested the staircase entrance from Sixth Avenue should be lowered so that people could see in and freely move through the park. All this allows the park to be more actively engaged with the street. Much like Jane Jacobs (with her ideas about "eyes on the street"), "Holly" Whyte believed safety comes from the public's active engagement with the street, not from fences.

Restoration and reinvention of the park landscape was the work of Laurie Olin, who, in keeping with Whyte's ideas, reestablished the importance of the central lawn by making it more accessible, with two new entrances, as recommended by Whyte. In addition, he changed pedestrian vantage points to make its unbroken expanse more visible from Sixth Avenue. Lynden Miller designed and planted two great three-hundred-foot-long borders of flowers along the north and south edges to replace overgrown hedges with a floral display of great seasonal splendor. Having been told "they" (the public) would destroy these gardens,

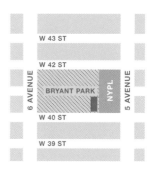

Marian Heiskell
Chair of the New 42nd
Street board of directors

MH: I remember so well sitting with Andrew in the citizen's group. We were having a big meeting as to whether or not Bryant Park could be turned over to a private group, because all the city parks belong to the public, to the city. And there was a big battle over this, and they finally gave in. And then of course they gave in on the Central Park Conservancy, and they've discovered that private groups can really do a lot more.

Everything was hidden in the park. I remember walking through it one day, and I came up to Andrew and said, "I just walked through Bryant Park." And he said, "You did *what*?" "Well," I said, "I wanted to see what it was like. Nobody accosted me; nobody tried to sell me drugs."

Daniel A. Biederman
President of the Bryant Park
Restoration Corporation

DB: I started when I was a kid, and I was just handed the job of turning Bryant Park around. You remember how terrible it was?

MF: Oh I remember—it was horrible. I never went there. I went to the front of the building to go to the library, but I never went in the back. How did you know what to do?

DB: I looked at Disney and Rockefeller Center, and I traveled

she insisted that if they were beautiful enough, "they" would keep and protect them. She was right.

Designing public spaces where people want to relax requires an understanding of what makes them feel comfortable. If the ambiance of a place gives people the sense they are being seen at their best, their enjoyment follows. They like to be able to choose, to believe they are in control of their movements and activities. A design environment that prescribes certain fixed routes—like the aisles of a supermarket or the long, blank corridors of a large hotel—offers little pleasure. In addition, for public spaces to feel lively and attract patrons, their activities must be consciously programmed. Both Rockefeller Center and Bryant Park are actively managed public spaces.

When the drug dealing that bedeviled Bryant Park in the 1960s spread to the front steps of the New York Public Library, it became clear the future of the two were inextricably linked. Their transformations began with an experiment: two temporary seasonal kiosks (built like scenery) were constructed on the library's front terrace to offer simple, unpretentious fare. People purchasing food, sodas, and coffee discouraged those whose illegal activities needed to be clandestine, and the former drug bazaar was supplanted by the commonplace activities of people enjoying their coffee breaks. The result was a new Fifth Avenue amenity, and the success of this experiment brought back the public to a location they had abandoned in fear.

Earlier plans for improving Bryant Park had included a spectacular proposal by Warner LeRoy (the former restaurateur of Tavern on the Green) to place a thousand-seat, domed, five-story glass pavilion on the terrace behind the library. It would have been visible from Sixth Avenue, dominating the west

Top Crystal Pavilion, 42nd Street, Manhattan, 1853

Bottom Bryant Park, Manhattan, 1932

Left The park's poorly maintained condition in 1970

a fair amount. Most of the good models weren't in New York.

William Hollingsworth Whyte, Jr., was a journalist for *Fortune* and wrote his own books, including *The Organization Man*, which you might have heard of. In the last twenty-five years of his life, he became the expert in the way people use public spaces. And his research was supported by the Rockefellers, both publicly and privately. A lot of the ideas behind Bryant Park initially came from him. We've since discovered how right he was on some of those things.

There was thought of having a second restaurant that matched, but once we built the grill (the indoor-outdoor building), we saw no reason to do that because the café was terrific. It was an outdoor, singles-action place spreading throughout the park. That was one of my ideas for adding activity to an unsafe park. It was going to replace the drug selling and drug using once going on along the rear wall.

We couldn't lower the park because the trees had been planted at this elevated level by Robert Moses, and they were fully rooted. There were new entrances added on the elevation of Carrère and Hastings's great marble building. LeRoy intended to control pedestrian access to the park through three entrances staffed by guards to ensure the capture of anyone who had engaged in misdeeds. Such an approach might seem efficient for preventing crime, but it would have effectively privatized a public park. Vigorous public debate about LeRoy's proposal gave the rear of the library sudden visibility; ultimately the scheme was rejected by the Landmarks Commission, which determined that it would overwhelm the building's west facade and its simple 297-foot-long pattern of vertical windows ending with pavilions at each corner.

<u>Above</u> Temporary food kiosk at the New York Public Library's east terrace, 1990

<u>Left</u> Bryant Park, 1995

The terrace beneath this facade was deeded as part of the library's ownership, so it is not legally a part of the adjacent 9.6-acre Bryant Park. When the city proved unable to provide sufficient financial support for operations, the park's land was leased—after great public debate—to a private entity, the Bryant Park Restoration Corporation. Andrew Heiskell, chair of the library's board of trustees, and Daniel A. Biederman oversaw formation of this corporation, which was empowered to supervise all the outdoor public space of the park. (This organization has since extended its influence to include both the Grand Central and Thirty-Fourth Street Partnerships, which are structured in a similar fashion on land also owned by the city.) Ownership of Bryant Park remains with the New York City Department of Parks & Recreation, and both organizations bear responsibility for its maintenance.

The cultural benefits of this public-private partnership, a common arrangement in New York City, are particularly evident in a project that complements the New York Public Library's public-service mission. The shared ownership, funding, and programming

south and north of the corridor that goes past the restaurant and grill, new entrances mid-block, and new entrances on the corner. So the accessibility, which was something Whyte obsessed about, was much improved.

MF: How has Hugh's work in the park changed the park?

DB: I think there's a certain great ambiance to the grill and café that makes people want to eat there—it's helped the success of the restaurants, which are important economic engines for the park. The combination of ipe (wood from South America), the glass, the way the windows work (they're normal, old-style windows that can open)—all of that is terrific.

MF: Do you do programs in the park?

DB: Yes, that's why Bryant Park works: the programming is what makes it so special. Knitting classes, concerts—you name it.

MF: So I could go over there and sit on a chair and just listen?

DB: Yes.

MF: Do I have to pay?

DB: Nope.

MF: Everything's free?

DB: The only things you pay for in the park are the carousel and the food. Everything else is free—all the programs.

responsibilities ensure a variety of changing seasonal uses, from ice skating to outdoor movies.

The agreement to permit large-scale income-producing activities on park land was an innovation, especially because lease agreements are with the private entity—the Restoration Corporation—not the parks department. This mix of commerce on land held in public trust has transformed the park from an abandoned, crime-infested eyesore to an extraordinarily active public space—one whose success has perhaps now led even to overuse. A balance must be struck between maintaining the park as a place for recreation or refuge and encouraging commercial activities to sustain its amenities. Meanwhile, private funding miraculously now even offers clean, attended public restrooms with baby-changing stations for both men and women, situated on the terrace owned by the library. The library now benefits from the seasonal mix of activities and services provided by the Restoration Corporation.

When presenting the design of the Bryant Park Café to the New York City Landmarks Preservation Commission, we suggested that the building was not intended to be architecture but rather an extension of the park, with vine-covered columns and open glass doors that would become part of the landscape of surrounding trees and shrubs. In fact, the latticework pergola structure now supports a year-round screen of vines, and in summer the roof is both a gathering place and a floral display. The kitchen was placed underground to allow for the construction of a second pavilion to the north of the Bryant *tempieto*. However, greater capacity (and more profit) are currently generated by using this space for a seasonal café, and so the existing pavilion continues to await its missing twin.

The project's overall success has been of great benefit to the surrounding community. Office rents have increased as a direct result of tenants' proximity to the park. Set against the imposing west facade of the white marble library, with a surrounding border of mature sycamore trees framing the great lawn that lies over five stories of underground book stacks, the restaurant and terrace have become one of New York's most active public spaces—a project that continues to be a great testament to Andrew Heiskell's public-spirited sagacity.

Bryant Park Café, west terrace

Lynden Miller
Designer of restored
Bryant Park gardens

LM: Hugh and I did the entranceway to the New York Botanical Garden, and we've done a lot of things together. I first met him in Bryant Park, when he did the temporary kiosks in front of the Public Library. He was clever enough to know that if you called them temporary, you could get them past the Art Commission. Those kiosks are now gone, but the ones in the park remain.

It turned out that Hugh understood and responded to what I was doing in Bryant Park (building two three-hundred-foot flowering borders, which incidentally don't now look anything like what I did, because they haven't been maintained. The plants are pretty overgrown, and our landscape in front of the library is gone.)

I believe in Frederick Law Olmsted and his philosophy that good parks are good for people. I saw what happened to people when they were surrounded by something beautiful, and they realized that it had been done for them—it was so moving.

Someone once said that gardening is the slowest moving of the performing arts. It's the public nature of these places, the fact that people need a connection with nature—when you give it to them, it changes them. It changes the way they behave, it changes neighborhoods.

Bryant Park

United States
Federal Courthouse
Jackson, Mississippi

H3 conceived this courthouse (built through the General Services Administration's Design Excellence Program) to celebrate its location and activities through an architecture rooted in place and responsive to Jackson's architectural heritage. The civic importance of the courthouse makes it worthy of special attention, so it has been given two commentaries in this book. The first section examined entry, an important ceremonial aspect of this significant civic structure. This second investigation, exploring public space, describes how the building offers the community a special experience in its different public gathering places.

Prominent views of the courthouse from the state capitol building dominate the eight-block-long axis connecting the two on Jackson's Congress Street, giving pedestrians arriving at the courthouse a clear route of access. A diagonal concrete wall displaying the Great Seal of the United States joins the building to Court Street, alongside a gently curving flight of outdoor stairs next to a wheelchair ramp. Both meet under a curving pergola that guides visitors to the front doors. This openwork structure is composed of an overhead trellis whose geometry completes the circular expanse of a six-story glass rotunda at the center of the building. Once inside, visitors are directed through a separate security area for inspection, then to an open, light-filled, one-story entrance ramp that feels welcoming and inclusive, not oppressive or authoritarian.

The eleven judges who work in this building bear ultimate responsibility for the structure's operation. The Honorable William H. Barbour, Jr., as the senior district judge, acted as representative of his fellow judges in making decisions about the building's design. In seeking to make architectural choices and to select artwork to complement the building's public spaces, how would we approach Judge Barbour and engage him in a dialogue about design, when so little representative contemporary architecture existed in the Jackson community?

We began an exchange about current ideas in art. To explain his preferences, Judge Barbour gave me

Les Shepherd
Chief architect for the General Services Administration

LS: The courthouse is directly on axis with the state capitol, immediately south of it. There is a void in the courthouse rotunda that forms a direct response to the capitol dome. This concave void makes an opposing gesture to the capitol's convex dome.

MF: How did Senator Daniel Patrick Moynihan's guiding principles for realization of federal architecture influence the project?

LS: The guiding principles cover everything from site selection to economical construction, and I think we met all those benchmarks. The courthouse is located within Jackson's central business district, which should allow it to enhance the life of downtown. And our value engineering guaranteed that we were using taxpayer money very responsibly. Perhaps the most memorable point in the guiding principles is that federal

a book of the spirited watercolors of Wyatt Waters, a local artist. They are deliciously vibrant images evoking the vivid flowers and foliage, colorful shadows, and intense heat of sun-drenched Jackson in summer. To investigate the power of abstract art and convey an understanding of what nonrepresentational imagery can offer, we took the judge and his wife, Stewart, to the Dia:Beacon art center on the eastern bank of the Hudson River. Here we explored the work of such abstract artists as Richard Serra, Dan Flavin, Sol LeWitt, Agnes Martin, and John Chamberlain.

We left Judge Barbour and his wife to their own pursuits and later encountered him in a gallery with two Bard College graduate students, notebooks in hand, who were discussing the work of Robert Ryman. Here was a room of blank canvases apparently representing nothing but the effort of applying white paint. Judge Barbour was nonetheless curious and asked the students for explanation. They immediately launched into a spirited presentation of their professor's theories: "This is an exploration about the nature of canvas and paint, about the essence of the act of painting," and so on. The judge listened intently, thanked them, and moved on, saying to us perceptively that these works had value only if you understood the lecture.

Months after this initial exploration of the intellectual side of contemporary art, a small committee convened to select three artists for the courthouse as part of the GSA's Art in Architecture program, dedicated to selecting contemporary artwork for its buildings. This jury included René Paul Barilleaux, chief curator of the McNay Art Museum in San Antonio, Texas, and Kathryn Kanjo, chief curator of the Museum of Contemporary Art San Diego, together with Judge Barbour and me.

Jeff Schmuki, a Jackson resident, was one of the artists chosen in our deliberations. Schmuki used the course of the Pearl River to create an abstract representation of the nearby stream along the entrance ramp's curving left wall. It accurately displays a convoluted meander in glazed tiles made from the stream's clay banks. This fanciful gesture brings visitors to their true point of arrival at the head of the ramp, on the main floor of the rotunda.

A second artwork, created by Seattle artist Katy Stone, accompanies the continuing sequence of entry. Installed below an eighty-foot-long skylight is

architecture should embody the finest contemporary thought and reflect regional architectural tradition simultaneously. Hugh accomplished both tasks, not only by responding to the state capitol in an ideological way but also by designing patterned features like ceramic frit coating on glass, trelliswork, and sun shading directly inspired by vernacular buildings.

Joseph Valerio
Peer reviewer on the General Services Administration's Design Excellence Program selection committee

JV: Jackson, Mississippi, is an icon of the South—a place key to the defense of Vicksburg in the Civil War, both part of tradition and a part of the region's future. In 2002 I was the GSA Peer on the selection committee for the architect of the new Federal Courthouse. An amazing range of architects from across the country was considered for the commission to design the building.

Should this be a firm from the region or one from a national practice? As decisions were made and the list was shortened, the committee looked for the right fit. In the end, the group was drawn to Hugh Hardy and his project architect, Daria Pizzetta. Here was a noted architect with a national and international reputation together with a highly talented young woman who, I later learned, grew up in a Bruce Goff–designed house in Louisiana. It was an inspirational team for an inspirational project that was both national and regional—both young and highly experienced, with leadership both intellectual and practical.

The outcome was a building with many positive civic dimensions. It aligns with the historic patterns of the city, while at same time symbolizes fundamental freedoms granted by our federal court system. It represents a tradition of high craft and excellence in construction. Being many different things for many different people, in the best tradition of American

a handsome and suggestive abstract metalwork in layers of painted, cutout aluminum sheets of different sizes and shapes. The work's transparency suggests the ephemeral: cloudscapes or the reflections in local lakes. At this rotunda level are elevator banks to deliver visitors to one of twelve courtrooms or on to other locations on the upper floors.

We chose a local artist, Fletcher Cox, to make six pairs of courtroom doors. Cox constructed them in part from pecan trees harvested from the site, designing a combination of split-faced panels and lightly sanded frames. These elements are put together to make twelve highly individual doors that authoritatively announce public access to the courtrooms.

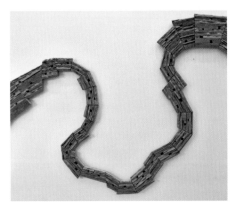 

Left *Pearl River*, Jeff Schmuki, 2010
Right *Cloudwaterline (horizon)*, Katy Stone, 2010

The initial team of artists had included a New Yorker who wished to include a political statement in his work, recognizing the importance of racial strife in the history of Jackson. The judges, however, did not wish to emphasize this aspect of the past, choosing instead to embellish the courthouse with Katy Stone's more welcoming, less confrontational artwork. Schmuki's river and Stone's cloudlike forms suggest nature, while Cox's doors celebrate the importance of this community facility through the use of site-specific material. The imagery of all three works is directly comprehensible, requiring no complex explanations or knowledge of past political events.

Access to an outside plaza formed by the rotunda offers relaxation on benches set in a landscape of local plants. Curving trelliswork and a pergola offer changing patterns of light and shade. These, together with one-story-high blue glass fins on the exterior of each connecting walkway level, offer small-scale variation to the large, six-story enclosing glass walls.

architecture, it is comfortable in its ability to define a place that celebrates our diversity.

William H. Barbour, Jr.
Senior judge for the Southern District of Mississippi

WB: We went around the country on a tour early on and viewed courtrooms in a number of places. Las Vegas has a courtroom that is famous for good design, and we went to Kansas City on the same trip. We sought out courtrooms in California. We went out to Cleveland, Ohio, to get ideas.

I enjoyed this whole process, and we found, much to my surprise, that throughout the whole history of our country there has been no standard design for a courtroom. And looking around the country at the different places where we went on our tour, the courthouses and the courtrooms themselves were all about the same. Even though there is no standard, they kind of followed the same idea about interior finishes. Every judge apparently has the idea that courtrooms should be big and magisterial and have lots of dark wood.

Hugh really did some interesting things with the courtrooms. He conceived the court process as theater, with the participants being the attorneys and the judge and the audience being the jury. So he developed this round design for the courtroom, which is, I think, pretty unique. The courtrooms have turned out to be very comfortable and very usable, and they work extremely well. A courtroom really ought not be just a big box, as they generally are. They ought to be working spaces, so everybody can see and hear. There should be enough room for the lawyers to work and the jury to be comfortably situated so they can pay attention. I think that's what we have produced here.

I have had a hard time hearing lawyers in the courtroom in the

This entry sequence is a layered experience that provides clear direction, as well as a succession of spatial events offering surprise and discovery.

Our courtrooms have greatly benefitted from an understanding of theater design. Participants' faces must be clearly visible and voices must be easily heard in a courtroom, just as in a stage performance. Although courtrooms traditionally use dark colors—heavy wood paneling and strong contrasts—to emphasize the importance, power, and majesty of the law, the results are often dark and gloomy, making faces hard to see. Good lighting is essential because one hears better if one can easily see the faces of those who speak. In Jackson, we have used a warm, light palette of textured stone, pecan wood, and fabric. Each member of the proceedings appears to equal advantage, presided over by the judge, who is given a raised position with central authority. We believe this approach has created a welcoming space where truth can be sought rather than a room intended for the sole expression of judicial power.

Due to its complex uses, the building contains three different circulation routes. One is for the public, one

past, but these courtrooms have absolutely phenomenal acoustics. In fact, the lawyers are complaining that you hear so well that you have to be very careful in talking with your client. The whispers carry. And the lawyers come up to the judge to speak about something—we call them sidebar conferences. Those conferences should normally be conducted right at the side of the bench, but the acoustics are so good that the jury can hear it, even though we've got white noise provisions to block that.

Fletcher Cox
Artist, designer, and fabricator of courtroom doors

FC: We were told the doors should be strong but not intimidating and, if possible, somewhat comforting. They were certainly going to be strong at three feet wide, eight feet high, and two-and-a-quarter inches thick, each made of pecan—one of our hardest and heaviest woods. So the search was for softness in a hard medium.

The first choice was to make the panels in split (raw) texture, laboriously desplintered and smoothed to achieve visual softness. The second was to make the doors patterned, rather than hierarchical, complementing the building's use of patterns. (By contrast, the traditional six-panel door configuration corresponds to the three zones of the human body in classical design.)

The first breakthrough was my decision to make the frame-to-frame area ratio in the new doors the same as that used in the previous courthouse. The second was to use a laminated structure. The third was to base the frame members on the log-cabin quilt design; I realized that I could use the contrast between heartwood and sapwood to define the joints between the strips and reinforce the log-cabin pattern, making the overall impression much stronger.

Then, over four years, we located thirteen downed pecan trees; cut them up; split, trimmed, and dried them; and milled them into panels.

for judges and judicial staff, and one for prisoners. However, all routes of circulation are simple and direct. Signage can therefore be minimal, with the main-floor elevator lobby offering a clear guide to all the floors of the building. In addition to secure surface parking for 107 cars, the building contains a secure 77-car garage divided into space for judges and staff.

We are privileged to have been chosen to create this statement about the rule of law. Although the design process was difficult, we had excellent resources in our project manager, Laura Shadix; our contractual client, the GSA (particularly Les Shepherd, chief architect); and the judges, who were unusually supportive of this investigation into contemporary architecture. I believe the building has been a welcome addition to the Jackson community and will continue in the future to represent the ideals with which it was created

Opposite **Federal Courthouse, atrium wall**
Top **Courtroom doors, Fletcher Cox, 2010**
Bottom **Courtroom interior**

But there was one more problem to be solved: pulls. For all my efforts to make comforting doors, they came out pretty tough, and they needed pulls of comparable presence. I made a couple of wood prototypes for casting that Hugh rightly rejected as too sweet. He said, "They need to show that they were made with some effort." And indeed they were. Month after month, ironworker and friend Rick Craft got up at 5:00 a.m. so he could maintain his stamina for the strenuous work without risking heart injury in the Mississippi heat.

Katy Stone
Artist for courthouse
entrance-ramp metalwork

KS: The initial inspiration for this work was a direct response to the architecture—the recurring use of horizontal line, layering, transparency, and translucency in the building. The architecture unfolds in an organic way, and I perceived a quality of lightness and airiness in the space. It felt as though the entire building seemed to invite the outside in. The main lobby, with its glass ceiling, asked for a work that interacted with light, something that reflected the clouds and sky and that spoke to the geography of the region. The relatively low ceiling also inspired a work that was horizontally expansive but had a subtle upward movement: something that felt like it was floating.

My work also responded to the open passageways. The main public spaces within the building are corridors with mostly glass walls, and people primarily experience the space in motion, passing through it on their way to the courtrooms. Acknowledging this, I incorporated directional light and painted and plain aluminum elements finished with different sheens so that when people walk by, the piece comes alive, shimmering and glinting. The shifting light in the space, the shadows and reflections from the natural and directional light, and the large arc of the curved wall all play a very important role in my artwork.

Continuity

"Restoration can be seen as
a dedication to clarifying each
structure's original character
combined with an awareness
of its current needs."

**Church of Saint
Luke in the Fields
New York, New York**

Conversation
Ledlie Laughlin
Former minister of
the Church of Saint
Luke in the Fields
and Roxana Laughlin

**Central Synagogue
New York, New York**

Conversation
Peter Rubinstein
Senior rabbi of
Central Synagogue

Projects

Church of Saint Luke in the Fields
New York, New York, restoration in 1985

Central Synagogue
New York, New York, restoration in 2001

"Continuity" contrasts two religious projects: an Episcopal church and a synagogue, permitting an exploration of the communal experience they have in common and the wide divergence of their stylistic approaches.

It is valuable to compare restorations of these two religious interiors, both of which followed disastrous fires. Each nineteenth-century building had been completely destroyed inside, losing its roof and most interior finishes. These catastrophes provided an opportunity not only to restore each worship space but also to rebuild it in a way that would serve contemporary ideas of their religious communities. In each case, the goal was to retain the building's original character while increasing its congregants' sense of involvement. Rather than reproducing exactly what existed before the fires, each renewal was designed to gather clergy and worshippers in a more intimate relationship. In both cases, we used new seating plans to create an immediate, personal experience while also questioning how to define the aesthetics of restoration. The widely diverging results demonstrate why one size does not fit all and show that to be successful, restoration's intent must be clearly defined.

The Church of Saint Luke in the Fields, founded in 1820, is the second-oldest Episcopal church building in Manhattan. As the congregation of St. Luke's grew, it called for increasingly elaborate services and Victorian design embellishment. The high-church aspirations of St. Luke's reached their zenith when the congregation moved to a new and expanded Romanesque home on 141st Street on the Upper West Side. It left its original building by the shore of the Hudson River to once again become a parish church. After a fire in 1981, only the walls of this structure were left standing. The presiding congregation then decided to abandon pretension and restore the simplicity and intimacy of the original Federal-style church. At the same time, the interior was adapted to reflect new ideas about the ceremony of worship that were advanced by the minister, Ledlie Laughlin. Although different in plan, the restored interior still enjoys the simplicity and spirit of the original.

Central Synagogue, built in 1873, is the oldest synagogue in continuous use in Manhattan. It had been raised in an optimistic outburst of decorative splendor but had seen its interior decoration greatly simplified in the aesthetic minimalism of the 1940s. This congregation also went back to the synagogue's origins, seeking in its restoration to re-create all the original polychromed splendor of 1873.

The synagogue's original decorative glories were still present in its ark (the vessel holding the sacred texts of the Torah), a miraculous survivor of the fire. A seating adjustment now permits Rabbi Peter Rubinstein flexibility when attendance varies, and entrance levels and stairs leading from Lexington Avenue were made less steep. But for the most part, this sixty-foot-tall interior features a painstakingly accurate re-creation of the original nineteenth-century decoration, a resplendent display of pattern and color.

Each place of worship retained its original character. But one pursued an increase in simplicity, the other a return to its original, colorful complexity. Restoration can therefore be seen as a dedication to clarifying each structure's original character combined with an awareness of its current needs. It is not a pursuit of fashion or make-believe but rather the serious investigation of joining a building's spirit to the requirements of contemporary activities.

Church of Saint Luke in the Fields New York, New York

My wife, Tiziana, and I were driving down the West Side Highway late one Sunday afternoon in 1981 when we heard on public radio that St. Luke's was at that moment suffering a disastrous fire. The roof was collapsing, the walls would soon stand in danger of failure, and its new organ and most of the furnishings were well on their way to total loss. When we reached the site, Ledlie Laughlin, the minister of St. Luke's, was standing dazed and disheveled in his slippers on the front sidewalk. Staring in disbelief at the building's destruction, he could scarcely even consider the effect it would have on future worship or on his recently successful efforts to make St. Luke's an independent congregation rather than a chapel of Trinity Church; all he saw was a scene of ruin. The next day the *New York Times* gave a sad account of the devastation this greatly loved community landmark suffered, announcing the walls might have to come down because they were unsupported and unsafe.

But these walls contained the history of this 1820 parish church, and their removal would inevitably lead to plans for replacement with a structure different from and more ambitious than the original. I therefore pleaded that the church (a community institution associated with our children's school) should rebuild in a way that would save this time-honored structure. Arguing for its importance in a planning and restoration process that ultimately included my services as architect, I was able to ensure that the sanctuary of the church was rebuilt on its original footprint.

But what should be rebuilt? The original parish church of 1820 (a chapel in the countryside on the shore of what was then called the North River) went undocumented except for a single woodcut. By the 1880s, poverty and decay comprised the salient character of the West Village, and the original St. Luke's congregation joined Manhattan's northward development and moved to 141st Street on the Upper West Side. The parishioners had plans to build a Romanesque church together with an impressive stone tower as a symbol of worship. (The tower was unrealized.) Left behind downtown was the old church, with its elaborate Victorian furnishings and a complex metalwork screen that separated worshipers

Ledlie Laughlin
Former minister of the Church of Saint Luke in the Fields and Roxana Laughlin

LL: Roxana and I were up with a group of kids in the country. A predecessor of mine had bought some property to make a camp for city children.

RL: You got a call in the middle of the night from a parishioner who said, "I'm looking down the street, and the church is burning." So then you drove down in the night.

LL: It was a long drive, I remember that. The strange thing was that we had just gone through a process to renovate the interior of the church, because it was filled with Victorian furniture. And there was this wonderful neighbor. One day we were having a meeting about plans to change the place, and she came to object. She didn't belong to the parish, but she was a concerned neighbor.

She said, "You want to remove all of these extra pieces of furniture. But I know how difficult it is to make my way to God, and this interior expresses it completely. Please don't fix it up."

The church is really a neighborhood setup. With the gardens and the school and the houses and the church, it is a great complex, and it was very much a community institution. And so, instantaneously, thousands of dollars came in after the fire without a request.

RL: The chapel over on the left had a beautiful altar from St. John's Chapel on Varick Street. When

from the high altar. These late nineteenth-century Gothic encumbrances, which were not part of the church's original simple interior, rose up against its western wall in an imposing, formal display that did not suit contemporary forms of worship.

Under Ledlie Laughlin's guidance, the separation between congregants and clergy had been changing prior to the fire. Laughlin had worked to enter into more informal and intimate relationships, making all feel welcome within his religious community. He sought to make Communion an intimate exchange by abandoning the distant, high altar and instead using a marble altar placed in a central location beneath a new ceiling oculus. The altar had been reclaimed from St. John's, a downtown chapel that was demolished in 1918.

Laughlin's desire to make the sanctuary less a preserve of the clergy helped to determine the direction of the restoration. He established the need for a small private chapel behind the altar. This intimate chapel with loose chairs is now located behind a screen detailed with a simple series of arches, where the alien Gothic decoration of the former high altar once loomed. In front of this are two formal bishop chairs set to face the Communion table. The altar platform was brought forward and raised three steps, which gives it more prominence and provides a place to kneel during Communion. This arrangement made clear the relationship of communion between worshipers and God as well as with each other.

Another change was to relocate the old baptismal font to a central position at the front of the church,

the church was demolished, the altar was brought up to St. Luke's. We made that into the main altar. I think that there was a rood screen—just sort of straight across—and the angels were on top of the rood screen. There were columns—Hugh brought them all out. And it speaks so much more of a wonderful space than it ever did before. Because it all had been sort of hidden back there.

LL: Yes, and the windows had all been dark. They were all Tiffany glass. Reds and blues, and so on.

RL: Hugh chose this wonderful new glass—dappled amber, and it moves from light to dark, so you get a sense of mystery. You're not particularly aware of it, but Hugh did that. It's wonderful. He ordered a gradation of light.

There was that initial feeling of: "Let's build it just the way it was." Well, Hugh said, "If you try and build it just the way it was, it will always be disappointing." It was the critical statement. And once he said that, the doors were open.

LL: In the old configuration, the altar was against the wall. And so the altar was brought forward, in order that the priest would celebrate from behind the altar, facing the congregation.

MF: And then congregants could come up and be close.

LL: Yes, but it was Hugh who established a platform coming out, and that was a great statement.

RL: I think so. There was really a sort of stage coming out.

LL: It was accessible. Inviting. Worship had been about the alone. That was sort of Victorian. And this is a new day, in which worship is the worship of a community. Not of a priest or choir, but of a community, and a community should be gathered together around the altar, which is the center. And so it was a great statement.

Trinity Church of Wall Street owned from the foot of Wall Street to Christopher Street on the West Side. It was Trinity's farm, given by Queen Anne for the establishment of Trinity Church.

under the choir balcony. Since baptism is primarily a family event, this setting—both prominent and intimate—makes the ritual more personal.

The entire sanctuary now invites participation. Before the fire, it had been distinguished by a colonnade that separated worshipers from clergy. Now it is open and embellished with a central arch that marks this as a place where congregants join together in communion. Two angels, miraculous survivors of the fire, adorn the two front corners and provide continuity between past and present. The result is a restoration of the intimate spirit of the original services rather than a re-creation of the past.

A new ceiling oculus brings down natural light to emphasize the altar below. Daylight illumination from the sidewalls' windows is made more effective by a series of hand-blown glass panes set within the original mullion pattern. Windows closer to the altar table are darker in color. At night the altar is emphasized by concealed electric illumination. Light is also provided by four chandeliers (not original to the building) in a conventional design that recalls the use of candles. All these manipulations are subtle, but they give the altar an appropriately prominent focus by day and night.

St. Luke's restoration and redesign shows the importance of accepting change as part of caring for landmark properties. Religious structures have value because of their associations with past tradition, but the surrounding community is what makes these buildings come alive, and the public must find them relevant to contemporary life. Otherwise these buildings, however beautiful, become abandoned monuments to past aspiration.

Donations for this project came even from those who did not regularly attend services. Fund-raising and construction were completed in only four years, making it clear that Laughlin's leadership had built strong community support. Today, the church has successfully reentered the life of the Village. Services are well attended, the neighboring gardens are cared for, and the school has a healthy waiting list. Restoration of spirit is particularly gratifying when rooted in a community with both a strong commitment to preservation and an abhorrence of pseudohistoric design. Within this context, hybrid design of St. Luke's has found comfortable acceptance.

Opposite Ledlie and Roxana Laughlin inspecting ruins after the fire, 1981
Above Restored rear elevation

St. Luke's was the northernmost piece. Amazing history.

RL: St. Luke's became independent and became St. Luke in the Fields.

LL: It had been the chapel of Trinity for over 150 years. It was called St. Paul's. Trinity had a forward-looking rector, and it set free its chapel and endowed it.

RL: But Hugh's building drew people. When it was finally rebuilt, it was just alive, and there was great rejoicing to come back into church and to enjoy a beautiful image. And I think the congregation was moved.

LL: Mrs. Astor was famous in New York for funding small things that she thought were important.

RL: And she had to go and see the things that she was going to fund.

LL: That's right—she would only give to something she had seen. And I said, "Of course." Well, one day, I was watching what was going on. There were workmen on the roof and one of them came sort of sliding down because this woman was on the sidewalk, right beside the church in process of being torn down. And he was frightened for this elderly woman walking right beside the building, and he came down to stop her and tell her that she should realize her danger. She said, "Oh, thank you. I'm just here because I want to give a million dollars." And he said, "Well, when you've given that, I hope you give me some change." And then he saw her silver Cadillac and thought, "Oh my God, who is this?"

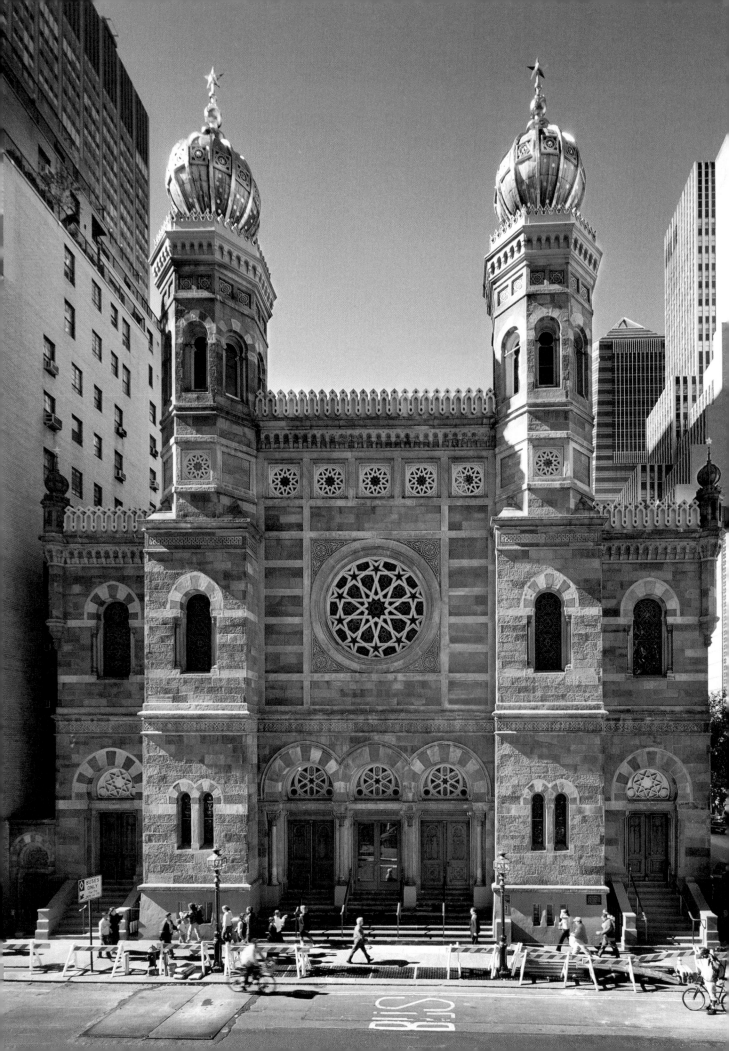

Central Synagogue
New York, New York

In 1998 Central Synagogue was engaged in a maintenance program, replacing its metal roof, when a small fire from a blowtorch (which workmen thought they had extinguished) smoldered over a weekend and burst into flame early one Monday morning. The dry wood trusses and roofing members caught fire and burned through before firemen could save the main roof. Fortunately, the ark holding sacred Torah scrolls, contained in a separate niche under a secondary roof, was saved. Only this, the wooden fascias of the balcony, and the tile floor, together with most of the stained glass, remained intact. Despite the fire department's uncommon care with the windows, water damage destroyed all interior plaster finishes.

Of all buildings constructed in late nineteenth-century New York, none conveys more optimism about future America than Central Synagogue. Realized in 1870 through 1872, a time of great economic expansion, it was consecrated before financial panic in 1873 and existed even before New York's two great museums, the American Museum of Natural History (1877) and the Metropolitan Museum of Art (which moved to its current site in 1880). The congregation at that time comprised only 140 families, but they were optimistic about growth for their congregation and erected a structure to house many times that number. Despite pressures to move uptown early in the twentieth century, the current site has been in continuous use for more than 140 years. Today it is one of a handful of landmark structures surviving from that era.

Although perhaps not a large building by today's standards, Central Synagogue has always graced the corner of Lexington Avenue and Fifth-Fifth Street with great authority. It proudly declares its presence in what was originally a residential neighborhood lined with four-story row houses. Built before Lexington Avenue was widened and the subway constructed below, it has stood resolute as the neighborhood was transformed into a vital part of the Upper East Side business district. Even juxtaposed with newer high-rise office buildings, it continues to be a distinctive presence.

Prior to the fire, Central Synagogue had not sustained the architectural changes St. Luke's underwent

Peter Rubinstein
Senior rabbi of Central Synagogue

PR: There's a sense that this building actually has the same flavor as it did when it was originally built. And a lot of the buildings on both sides of the street on Fifty-Fifth—the brownstones—are in keeping with what this neighborhood looked like then.

We went to the membership and said, "If you had to change one thing, what would it be?" and they said, "the steps leading up to the building." Because the steps were so narrow and high that when you walked out—especially if you couldn't walk quickly—there was a sense that you were cascading down. Hugh decided to lower the entire lobby floor so that it could be one level, and it could be a bit of a gathering space.

MF: How much of the original building was still here after the fire?

PR: Just the four walls; the ark, because that's under a separate roof; and the pillars, because they're cast iron. The pews were destroyed. The roof had caved in. There probably were seven trusses that held up the roof. One of them collapsed—caved in—and actually speared right down through the floor to the floor below.

MF: Were you at the synagogue at that point?

PR: I wasn't, but I actually did come in with one of our contractors. There was a Torah still in one of the cases, and I broke the glass and took it out. I don't think I was in danger, but the fire department

through the years, but the visual appearance of its interior had been significantly altered from its original design. Its stenciled walls bore the revised interpretation of Ely Jacques Kahn, a congregant and prominent architect of the mid-twentieth century. In 1949 he supervised a complete repainting of the interior, simplifying patterns and toning down colors. The result was a pale semblance of the original, in keeping with popular taste of the 1940s.

Far Left Central Synagogue, 1872
Left Stencilwork after the 1949 repainting
Above Fire damage to roof, 1981
Opposite Restored stencilwork

We were able to document the original patterns and colors with the assistance of DPK&A, an architectural firm in Philadelphia. Since total resurfacing was called for, no effort was made to restore the midcentury color scheme. Instead, we sought to re-create the all-encompassing vibrancy of the original decoration.

Those patterns originated with the traditions of early Jewish nomads who used tents made of fabric and rugs for worship. Restoration required hundreds of stencils faithfully copied from the original artwork by DPK&A and cut from Mylar, with paint applied by brush using traditional techniques. To recall the random texture of fabric, a plaster finish was mixed with sand, and paint was deliberately applied with an uneven texture. Members of the congregation were asked to make their own individual stencils; each contribution was symbolic of the complete restoration. The only new addition was a scattering of gold stars across the brilliant blue ceiling (an element for which there is much historic precedent, even though there was no proof of its use at Central Synagogue).

Although the stencilwork was to be as bright as the original, did this mean that all other interior finishes should follow suit? This would certainly dazzle every eye, but how would it affect historic continuity?

was very upset that I had done that. But by that point, I was safe, and the Torah was safe.

MF: What started the fire?

PR: We were redoing the building over the course of several summers. We were putting in air conditioning. Some workmen were putting in flashing—copper—and instead of using hot tar, which was specified, they used a blowtorch to heat the tar behind it. And what they forgot— or didn't think of—was that behind that outside stone wall there is wood that was 130 years old. So it caught and the fire spread up to the roofline, and between the roof and the ceiling—it just spread like a wildfire. The fire department knew that if the fire dropped into the walls where there's wooden latticing, the building would collapse. So they actually created a horizontal water-wall from the clerestory windows. That's what saved the walls. If more than a few of those trusses had gone, the walls would have just caved in.

What Hugh did was create a sense of *aliyah* (the Hebrew word for "ascent"). When you walk in, you're actually ascending, translating the Jewish tradition of *aliyah* into the physical experience of entering the sanctuary.

This was not a brand-new building, and to restore all its surfaces in the name of complete accuracy would require bleaching wood and reinstalling gas illumination. But this approach would deny the building's full history. The key to this history lay with the colors of the ark (made of oak contrasted with fir) and all the balcony woodwork. These muted survivors had darkened with age, giving the interior an aura of authority. Instead of bleaching these surfaces back to an imagined original color, we refinished them without chemicals, retaining variations and individual wood-grain patterns. Gilding on the columns framing the ark's enclosure was similarly muted.

Stained-glass windows set in both the high and low walls of the building boldly manipulate light. Their original fanciful colors, most particularly a deep, radiant blue, set this room apart from the outside world. Worshippers enter a space transformed by colored light and illuminated by twelve reconstructed chandeliers and ten smaller hanging fixtures. These various light sources dematerialize the interior, making it appear as insubstantial as a tent.

The restored Central Synagogue embodies contemporary ideas of worship, offering a less formal experience. Rabbi Rubinstein can now move the first thirteen rows of upholstered benches at the front of the sanctuary to change their configuration at times of year when attendance is low and he wants to gather people more closely together. On occasion, by bringing the lectern forward from its platform on the bema down to the main floor, he can address a smaller congregation in a more intimate setting. The renewal of this synagogue under Rabbi Rubinstein's leadership thus combines a respect for tradition with an openness to contemporary forms of worship.

Everything is new except for the tiles that are in the aisles. We picked up every tile that we could save, and we catalogued them—tiles do okay in fire. We put them back down in the aisles— not exactly where they had been, because we had to piece them together. Then we went back to the company that had made them originally, and they created new tiles. You previously had to step up about four inches when you entered the pews, because the original hot water heating ran underneath. We were able to lower the pews to make the floors one level.

We wanted flexibility built into the sanctuary. Because one of the things that we had learned over time was that it is impossible to know what the future will need. We wanted something a little more informal, which is the way it is now.

During most of the year, we remove the front; the center platform slides out. We can flip this sanctuary into at least two major configurations. The side pews had been all facing straight forward. The relationship between the pulpit and the ark is now very different. There's a greater sense of informality, plus huge visual access to the ark.

We decided to go back as close to the 1870s feel as we could. The original windows were on the top tier. They were much simpler and much paler. When it's sunny, it's amazing to see how the ark gets bathed in light. It is just showered with light.

We also made sure we had the highest level of technology. So we livestream our services, and you can see the cameras around. The other thing Hugh did was to drop four microphones.

The sanctuary was all hand-painted by our members. There's a tradition in the Torah that if you write one letter you've written the complete Torah. So I said, "I want that here, so that everyone can say: 'I built the building.'" And we put up little platforms so that even little kids can all remember. They can all point to which stencils they did. So there's a human element to this.

Environment

"The real issue in intelligent use of resources is how to promote a philosophy that considers buildings part of nature, not independent manmade elements."

**Alice Busch Opera Theater
The Glimmerglass Festival
Cooperstown, New York**

Conversation

Paul Kellogg
Former general and
artistic director of the
Glimmerglass Opera

**Botanical Research
Institute of Texas
Fort Worth, Texas**

Conversations

Sy Sohmer
Director of the Botanical
Research Institute of Texas

Edward Bass
Vice chair of the Botanical
Research Institute of Texas

"Environment" compares an upstate New York opera house with a botanical-research institute in Fort Worth, Texas, to explore different responses to environmental issues and methods of energy conservation.

Of all the issues that confront contemporary architecture, our wasteful consumption of resources and accelerating need for electrical power are among the most urgent. Buildings consume more than 30 percent of all the forms of energy combined and more than 60 percent of all the electricity used in the United States every year. Although Leadership in Energy and Environmental Design (LEED) certification has greatly raised consciousness about "green" buildings, much of what it addresses are common-sense concerns such as site orientation and the use of energy-efficient mechanical equipment and nontoxic materials. But the real issue in intelligent use of resources is how to promote a philosophy that considers buildings part of nature, not independent manmade elements.

The Alice Busch Opera Theater at the Glimmerglass Festival is open to the public during only two or three summer months a year. To gather people together in this beautiful, rural site in an enclosed environment with mechanically controlled temperature and humidity would have been absurd. Such a structure would cut off audiences from outdoor breezes and views. Upstate New York in summer continues to offer sufficiently mild evenings (despite fears of global warming) that this performance hall can withstand outdoor conditions without mechanical refrigeration. Therefore the total experience of arrival, anticipation, performance, and dispersal can take place without any large-scale energy-consuming mechanical equipment.

In Fort Worth, Texas, the Botanical Research Institute of Texas (BRIT) contains a twenty-thousand-square-foot climate-controlled herbarium. It is home to more than a million dried plant specimens used by scholars and scientists to study botany. This special archive requires a complete BRIT's

Projects

Alice Busch Opera Theater
The Glimmerglass Festival
Cooperstown, New York, 1997

Botanical Research Institute of Texas
Forth Worth, Texas, 2012

complete mechanical system, but it also uses geothermal wells to provide year-round fifty-degree liquid for heating and cooling. Little additional heat in winter and only reduced mechanical refrigeration in the summer are needed. These same systems preserve the herbarium's seed collection and provide acceptable working conditions for the staff in the forty-four-thousand-square-foot two-story building. Staff and public areas feature the use of operable windows. Because this project is a visible manifestation of environmental awareness, all operational aspects of the building are visible to the public, from onsite water management to vine cladding on the exterior to a fully developed green roof that also includes areas for solar cells.

The design philosophies of both projects establish them as a part of nature and as examples for educating the public about more benign ways to use natural resources.

Alice Busch Opera Theater
The Glimmerglass Festival
Cooperstown, New York

This brave project was the vision of the opera's artistic director, Paul Kellogg. Constructed in 1987, it stands a 190-mile drive from New York City on the shores of Lake Otsego, near Cooperstown, New York. From modest beginnings as a seasonal company offering performances of opera in English at the local high school, Glimmerglass Opera was shepherded into prominence as an internationally recognized company that combines a professional orchestra and a local chorus with principal singers recruited from New York City. Under the current leadership of critically acclaimed artistic director Francesca Zambello, it is increasingly known for the success of its Young Artists Program, originated by Kellogg. This is an ambitious and inventive company whose loyal audiences enjoy well-sung, inventively staged, and accessible productions of opera classics. This saga represents an unusually successful professional achievement.

The original venue of the company, the Cooperstown High School auditorium, suffered from poor sightlines and muffled acoustics. There was no orchestra pit, and a low ceiling and a proscenium with the proportions of a letter slot had been designed to save money. Sopranos' best sounds would soar up into the rafters, bypassing the audience. It was Paul Kellogg who, despite the risk, urged his trustees to abandon this auditorium and build a new opera house up the lake.

Cooperstown was then noted more for the National Baseball Hall of Fame than for high-quality music performances, and the conundrum of how to raise money for this radical plan seemed insolvable. Cooperstown, however, has unusual private resources for a rural community, and it was hoped that summer residents who loved opera might be willing to support a summer festival. Construction of the opera house ultimately was made possible by Tom Goodyear, who donated land that was once the site of his turkey farm, together with Alice Busch. The entire project was guided by a spirit of collaboration and the sure knowledge that we were creating something special.

An open, fanciful site plan was developed, combining new construction with existing farm structures to make the rural environment an integral part of the

Paul Kellogg
Former general and artistic director of the Glimmerglass Opera

PK: The opera's first performances were in 1975. It was founded as a summer opera company—because that's when the audience is here, or can get here. (The winters up here are pretty severe.) At that time it was performing in the local high school. I became associated with it in 1976, when my partner, Raymond Han, was asked by the director of the company to do sets for a couple of productions.

Raymond had never done a stage set in his life, and he was reluctant to get involved. But he did two beautiful productions, which were well received, and then he decided he would never do another stage set again. There are just too many people involved. Everybody's got an opinion, and Raymond was used to working as a studio artist—an easel artist. And no one was allowed in his studio. But when you start doing something like that, it becomes a much more public process.

MF: How did you get from the high school to the current location?

PK: It's a big, big, big story. I'd worked as a volunteer for the company, so I'd gotten to know people during the summers when Raymond was painting the sets. I was helping him, and then I started doing props, so I

opera-going experience. Following an earlier attempt to construct a formal, concrete structure shaped like a shopping center and set in a paved parking lot, the new hall was instead built of steel and wood and set in an open landscape containing a small pond that feeds its sprinkler system. With pledges for financial donations in place, the new nine-hundred-seat opera house was designed in the form of a large barn that harmonized with the landscape.

In thinking about the design, I was inspired by Cooperstown's hay and cattle barns, whose distinctive sloping roofs fit so well into the landscape. These forms are also found in the industrial landscape of Pittsburgh's steel mills. Around the same time, Tiziana and I were staying with Isamu Noguchi in Takamatsu, Japan. He generously took us on a six-hour drive to view one of Japan's oldest Kabuki theaters, on the island of Shikoku. Imagine my surprise to discover that this elegant wood building, located on a remote part of the island, was made of the same basic set of forms found in the Cooperstown barns! How startling that the common need for natural ventilation shared by barns, steel mills, and theaters over the centuries would lead to an almost identical set of traditional section profiles.

The electrical energy required to cool a nine-hundred-seat auditorium would be substantial if sufficiently large quantities of refrigerated air were to circulate slowly enough to meet acoustical criteria. The costs of building, maintaining, and operating such an artificially cooled structure (which would be occupied only a few months each year) would be financially unsustainable as well as environmentally unsound.

Architectural responses to environmental issues have taken many high-tech forms, but this project was built around a direct and simple approach to energy conservation. A two-tiered auditorium houses a festival theater that uses only natural ventilation instead of mechanical cooling. Its open design of eight two-story sliding doors (supplemented by visible ceiling fans) permits natural breezes to dissipate heat without any refrigerated air, bringing audiences closer to nature. Opening or closing the moving walls are the only responses that can be made to changing weather; demands for electrical power are therefore far less than those of a conventional auditorium.

But how could our client be convinced to pursue such an unconventional approach, even in the name of cost savings? We cited the music shed

got to know a lot of people in the company. In a couple of years, the company ran into some problems—some personality problems. The board, members of whom I'd known around town, asked me (because I had some administrative experience) if I'd be interested in temporarily helping out part-time with managing the company, since they were losing their director.

So I did. And eventually it became a kind of passion—and there were a number of people at that time on the board who were equally passionate about Glimmerglass. And we all decided that the thing to do was to see if we could move out of the theater and get a new place to perform. And so we got excited about building something, and there was a long process where we were concerned about the money and about where to go and all of that.

But a board member, Tom Goodyear, had a large property up the lake. His mother owned it, and he said, "I'll just get my mother to donate some land to Glimmerglass—about forty acres."

Hugh came up with a design that could be accommodated by our budget. "Procession" is the word he used often. It was a great, enlightening expression for me. We talked about the procession for the audience. That means how the audience arrives at the building and gets in the building, how it is focused.

Hugh felt very strongly that there should be no parking between the road and the building, which is absolutely the right thing. There

Alice Busch Opera Theater, circa 1987

at Tanglewood, in the Berkshires region of Massachussetts, and other outdoor performance venues such as the Opera Theatre of Saint Louis as proof that nature could be an ally.

In practice, the experience of leaving one's car behind on a hillside parking lot to walk around a pond and through pastoral grounds to reach the open opera house has offered an important passage for audiences. Inside the auditorium, before the overture starts, views of a gentle, rural landscape can still be seen through the open side walls. Then, the two-story sliding panels slowly close to focus attention on the stage, completing the theatrical transition from one world to another. Such a carefully choreographed sequence from parking to performance would not be so successful if it ended in a fully sealed, mechanically refrigerated auditorium.

Even in a project where every penny counts, important elements of the design survived because Paul Kellogg was brave enough to support us. The building's entry is announced by a pair of sixty-foot-tall flagpoles that flaunt striped pennants. Their animation heralds stray breezes and emphasizes nature's presence. In short, everything possible is done to make this gathering place a part of its site rather than an alien imposition. It ensures that the experience of performances at Glimmerglass changes not only with what is presented onstage, but also through occurrences in the natural environment. Even thunder and lightning can become surprise performers, lending unexpected drama to onstage events.

Although the future economic health of performing arts in America remains in doubt, and Glimmerglass annually struggles in a rural area immersed in economic hardship, loyal audiences have kept the opera alive for thirty-seven years and are determined to see it continue. Music critics claim the one great asset of the company (aside from its astonishing record of outstanding performances) is the opera house itself. Considered an excellent place to perform, its open site and intimacy are also much appreciated by audiences. It has changed and enhanced the many lives associated with the company and continues to add exceptional memories to its history of accomplishment.

were people who felt that it would be inconvenient to have people parking across the road and having to walk, but it's so important to the whole experience of that place. As you approach the building, you are making a little effort to get there, and it becomes a part of the process of getting ready for a performance. So you approach the building, and you go inside the building. The sides are open, and you take your seat and face the stage, but you're chatting and so forth. And then, slowly, the doors begin to move forward, and you become aware that something's happening. The building itself is moving, and it's drawing your attention toward the stage, moving from back to front.

MF: When the walls move, do they completely enclose the space or is there always some open area?

PK: In a performance you cannot really have any ambient light— you have to be able to close down the space completely so that the stage lighting can have an effect. So it closes completely, and stage lighting takes over. So, suddenly, you are finding yourself in an enclosed theater with your attention and your expectations all focused on what's happening in front of you on the stage and in the orchestra.

MF: So it's a normal proscenium opening?

PK: A normal proscenium was actually more useful for what we did than just a kind of black-box opening. That's good for certain kinds of theater, but not for opera particularly. Opera's been around for four hundred years, and it's worked very well on a proscenium stage. It is a form designed for prosceniums. I think this one particular kind of theater needs it.

Hugh understands so much about the theater. He just gets it. You sense immediately when you're dealing with him that he understands it.

Botanical Research Institute of Texas Fort Worth, Texas

Our current generation is facing an educational challenge of immense dimensions. Although the interlocking ecosystems that sustain life on this planet are becoming better understood, they are not always well served. Profit motives have become so powerful that long-term damage is being done to our land and biosphere without regard for the welfare of future generations. The time for a greater awareness of environmental issues among all levels of the population is at hand. In Fort Worth, Texas, the Botanical Research Institute of Texas (BRIT) has been created to generate just that awareness.

BRIT is fortunate to have constructed its new building in a time when the public is becoming aware of the changing natural environment. Americans and the international community are increasingly mindful of the need to use the planet's finite resources wisely, to find new ways to cultivate renewable forms of energy, and to challenge the wastefulness of disposable products. BRIT's exploration of the natural world through field study, scientific research, botanical analysis, and educational programs is highly noteworthy.

Americans have become used to ignoring the cycle of the seasons, preferring instead the comforts of year-round climate control. We like to live with constant temperature and humidity, ignoring the gifts from the heavens of shifts in sun angles; moving leaf patterns; and the flowering and decay of grasses, trees, and shrubs—all responses to seasonal change. Only in the desert is one day exactly like the next. By contrast, we hope that in its exploration of the natural environment, BRIT will offer ever-unfolding discoveries.

BRIT's new structure uses exemplary methods of landscape design, water management, energy use, site placement, and material selection—all warranting a Leadership in Energy and Environmental Design (LEED) platinum rating from the US Green Building Council. Every aspect of construction, from rainfall management to window orientation, has been monitored to ensure the smallest possible environmental impact.

Sy Sohmer
Director of the Botanical Research Institute of Texas

SS: BRIT is basically a conservation organization, and we work through what I call three *d*'s: discovery, documentation, and dissemination. We discover plant life and plant diversity; we document it through our collections; and we disseminate the information we gather through research publications, books, and a very powerful education and outreach program that takes information about BRIT and what we do into the community as well as into national arenas.

I want to point out that we are unique, because we are a freestanding organization—the only herbarium in the country not associated with a museum or university. But what we do is exactly the same thing that all other herbariums do. Most of them are small: very few of them have more than twenty to thirty thousand specimens.

Our area of research is called "systematics" or "taxonomy." It's documenting plant diversity, trying to discern the relationships between these species and where they're located (their "biogeography"). We want to be working in areas where the greatest amount of plant diversity still exists. When I was an assistant director of the Bishop Museum in Honolulu in the 1980s, 6 to 8 percent of

BRIT's origins lie with the Fort Worth Botanic Garden, built in 1934 on 109 acres of land given by the city of Fort Worth. It has since grown to include twenty-five hundred different species, which are displayed in twenty-one specialty gardens. In 1987 Southern Methodist University (SMU) joined its 75,000-volume botanical library with Vanderbilt University's herbarium of 360,000 plant species to create the Botanical Research Institute of Texas. This institution sponsors research programs in the Amazon, New Guinea, and the Andes, acting as a single resource for the study and enjoyment of botany under the energetic leadership of Dr. Sy Sohmer.

BRIT has become a complementary neighbor to the Fort Worth Botanic Garden through a close coordination of programming. BRIT provides a scientific counterpart to the aesthetic and educational assets that the nearby institution has long enjoyed. Its landscape, building, and technology systems will advance public understanding of conservation practices and the intelligent use of our diminishing natural resources.

<u>Top</u> Botanical Research Institute of Texas, front door and canopy
<u>Bottom</u> Flexible compact shelving

the Philippines was still covered with old-growth forest. There is none today, as far as I know. Many of the species that were collected during the Philippines flora project that I originated at the museum and brought to the Botanical Research Institute no longer exist in the wild. The only record of their existence is the kind of specimens that we collect. And of course you don't collect in single batches—you collect in duplicates and you spread those duplicates around. You trade with other like organizations.

<u>MF</u>: How did you divide the spaces that constitute BRIT?

<u>SS</u>: Hugh Hardy said, "OK, you do two things: you do collections—that's the specimens and the library—and you do the research and education, et cetera." And at that moment, the concept of two separate but attached buildings came to be. Collections have to be kept in a climate-controlled space. The Archive Block doesn't have any windows on the sides for that reason; the building expresses the actual function of BRIT. We have the documentation represented by the library and specimens, and the dissemination represented by research and education.

The main issue with collections is keeping cigarette beetles out, because the larvae of the cigarette beetle can really destroy dry plant material very quickly. And that is why you have climate control. It's not unique to this place—it's just that we happen to have probably the most cutting-edge facility in the world right now for collections of this nature.

But this is not a mausoleum with a sealed atmosphere. It's sealed, of course, and well air-conditioned, and the space is kept about ten degrees cooler than the rest of the building. But we bring tours in there all the time. Now, when researchers come to use the collections, they choose the specimens that they are working with, bring them outside to an adjacent space, and work on them there.

Everything we use here is renewable. The ceilings are bamboo, and the flooring is

BRIT's new structure presents nothing less than a case study in conservation. The site's prominent position near a major Fort Worth thoroughfare, University Drive, offered the opportunity to design a building that could visibly represent a philosophy of environmental responsibility. But how could this be established in architectural terms?

Primarily, we situated the building in the context of the landscape rather than as a freestanding structure, placing it carefully with regard to sun angles. The two-story complex is organized in two volumes. Herbarium and support-staff areas are contained in the "Archive Block." We created roofs and walls out of poured-in-place, almost windowless tilt-up concrete panels to reduce fuel consumption in manufacture and transportation. These roofs and walls are integrated with plant life, hosting a tapestry of native species that acts as a gentle living embellishment. In addition, the herbarium roof contains a hidden field of photovoltaic panels that generates enough electricity to power building lights.

The other volume, the "Think Block," contains administrative, educational, and research functions, along with other public activities. This section is enclosed by precast concrete panels with windows that are shielded on the west and open glass on the north. A sloping roof features patterns of native plants integrated with the surrounding landscape.

Because BRIT is both a scientific and an educational institution, every aspect of its design and construction has been considered in response to environmental issues. The project has been designed with the latest sophisticated mechanical and electrical systems, which maintain a variety of working and study environments. The herbarium's study collections (as well as the comfort of employees) demand year-round control of temperature and humidity, in a Texas climate where annual temperature averages more than 70 degrees and average humidity ranges from approximately 60 to 80 percent. The system includes 168 geothermal wells that use groundwater for heating and cooling. Throughout, we strove to create a building with uncommonly efficient mechanical and electrical systems that would foster occupants' awareness of site, orientation, fenestration, and materials.

terrazzo, which was actually salvaged from the building that we tore down to make space for our building. That cement was reused in the terrazzo flooring. A lot of the building, especially the Think Block, has wool carpeting, because sheep grow wool all the time. It's not artificial. Some of the floors in the education area—especially in the herbarium—are made from recycled rubber and sneakers. These are all renewable materials—that's part of why we're a LEED platinum building.

There were four or five thousand people here for the opening. We weren't really planning on making a business of renting out the facility, but we've gotten so many requests. I don't know how many weddings there have already been in this building since we opened to the public last May. So it's obviously very popular. It's certainly given us a much higher profile.

MF: Have you been able to add to your collection since you've had the larger space?

SS: No herbarium stops growing. If it stops growing, it's a dead herbarium.

Edward Bass
Vice chair of the Botanical Research Institute of Texas

MF: What in your background fostered your passion for the environment?

EB: I think it started growing up with my dad. My dad was a great outdoorsman. He was a cattle rancher, fisherman, bird hunter, and really had a passion himself. We grew up with that, my brothers and I.

MF: How did you get involved with BRIT?

EB: BRIT grew out of the collections—the herbarium and botanical library—of SMU. They were moving toward deaccessioning those collections. They were going to be dispersed principally between Missouri and the New York Botanical Garden.

Those arriving at BRIT enter through a varied landscape. First, a circular drop-off leads to a curving trellis that shelters visitors and announces the front door, located at the midpoint of the Think Block. From here, cars park in curving, tree-shaded ranks. Next, from this entrance, a stunning view opens down a 210-foot-long corridor that runs the length of the building to its eastern end. Inside the main hall, a two-story glass wall looks out to the north over a newly planted prairie that evokes the original Texas landscape, awash with bluebonnet flowers in spring. In this large hall, a sloping bamboo ceiling intersects a curving wall finished with recycled random lengths of sinker cypress. These boards were dredged from underwater, milled, and interspersed with low-voltage amber LED light strips. A curving switchback stair set with rusted metal panels has a textured, natural character. This use of reclaimed material dramatizes BRIT's dedication to a careful use of natural resources.

Imaginatively designed by Diana Balmori, the institute grounds and building surfaces enjoy several innovations. Jointly sponsored by the City of Fort Worth and BRIT, a landscaped parking area for both the Botanic Garden and BRIT replaces the typical black macadam expanse so inhospitable in Texas heat. Cars are parked on a paved, tree-lined field whose sloping surface leads groundwater to an onsite water-retention pond forming part of a children's study garden. BRIT and the Botanic Garden share a walkway of braided, native plant species whose botanical display provides a horticultural introduction for visitors.

Not only has the building achieved the highest LEED rating, its landscape thoughtfully educates the public about the environment. By further including plant life as an integral part of its design, the building's architecture becomes part of the natural landscape, encouraging visitors to contemplate how construction can improve, not harm, the planet.

A small group of people in this area found out about it and thought it was important they remain in the region. They founded BRIT, and SMU would agree if they could find a permanent home for the collections and a means of supporting them. The assumption was that they would remain in the region as a collaboration between BRIT and SMU. And so, a little delegation of about six or seven people came to visit me at my office. They figured I must have an interest in botany. I was the first person they talked to over several months' time to whom they did not have to explain what a herbarium was.

We spent two decades moving toward building the building. When we got to the point in the process where we had some money, and we had a game plan, we started looking for architects.

I really got to know Hugh when we were in the process of selecting an architect. Hugh was among, I think, about a half a dozen that we looked at closely. He had worked at the New York Botanical Garden. He understood the Botanical Garden. I always thought his visitor's center was quite wonderful. That very much impressed us, but we had architects representing various approaches and styles. Essentially, we had a long-term planning committee that was charged with the job of moving forward the building project. And I think there was a consensus that we would move toward a modernist approach as opposed to a very traditional building. I was happy with that. I've got experience with both directions.

BRIT was founded with the concept that its collections would be affiliated with various institutions in the region—SMU, of course, being one of those. And we continue a close relationship with SMU and some of its scientists. Also Texas Christian University and the University of Texas, Arlington. We have close relations with the University of North Texas Health Science Center. The Fort Worth Botanic Garden did not have a botanical science wing, as really all great botanic gardens do. BRIT was designed

Top East elevation
Middle Green roof
Bottom Diana Balmori's
rendering of the east wall

to provide that resource, together with the Dallas Arboretum.

Our outreach in education is very considerable, and we are located on a piece of city land. We leased about five acres from the city next to the Botanic Garden. Our new building and the landscaping that is part of it expanded their campus.

MF: Did you work with Diana Balmori on her part of the project?

EB: Yes we did. That was a great collaboration. A lot of it was keyed into this concept of living plants used all along the exterior walls of the building. Those that were built by the tilt-wall system are designed to be covered eventually with a variety of climbing plants. Botanists are experts in dealing with the herbarium collection of over a million sheets, each mounted with parts and pieces of dead plants. This organization is now faced with maintaining living walls on buildings. It's all going to work great, but it's interesting and amusing that the botanists' world has been expanded into horticulture.

The green roof was a wonderful collaboration. Tony Burgess, an ecologist at TCU who has a tremendous interest in and knowledge of the prairie lands around the Fort Worth region, headed up the research: What do you plant? How would you make an indigenous area on the roof? He calls it "biomimicry." The particular plants, the soil structure, and so forth, are found on certain areas of the Fort Worth prairie called the barrens. They are the rocky tops of hills; the plants there are adapted to thin soil, drought, and dry conditions, because the rain immediately runs off. Our roof is a piece of Fort Worth prairie barrens. Tony Burgess carried out the research, with his graduate students doing all sorts of trials and plantings in different soils and different plants and so forth. That in itself was a fascinating collaboration. It advances the whole concept of green roofs—they aren't just places where you plant Bermuda grass or something like that. Living roofs can become part of the local natural system.

Intimacy

"For the most part, young audiences exist in a different culture from that of older generations. It is in small performance spaces containing only a few hundred seats where these new, younger audiences can be found."

The Claire Tow Theater at Lincoln Center New York, New York

Conversations
Bernard Gersten
Executive producer of
Lincoln Center Theater

André Bishop
Artistic director of
Lincoln Center Theater

Richard B. Fisher Building, Brooklyn Academy of Music Brooklyn, New York

Conversations
Joseph Melillo
Executive producer and
artistic director of the
Brooklyn Academy of Music

Karen Brooks Hopkins
President of the Brooklyn
Academy of Music

Theatre for a New Audience Brooklyn, New York

Conversation
Jeffrey Horowitz
Founding artistic
director of Theatre
for a New Audience

The Claire Tow Theater at Lincoln Center
New York, New York, 2012

Richard B. Fisher Building,
Brooklyn Academy of Music
Brooklyn, New York, 2012

Theatre for a New Audience
Brooklyn, New York, 2012

"Intimacy" describes three small theaters for institutional clients in New York City. Each shares goals for audience development and scale of theatrical production, together with similar small capacity, but the architectural results differ greatly.

For the most part, young audiences exist in a different culture from that of older generations, whose lives continue to be circumscribed by tradition: eating three set meals a day, wearing certain socially prescribed clothes for defined activities that occur in specific places. Their entertainments take place in traditional venues, with subscriptions bought a year in advance; their public eating occurs in restaurants. Their late-nightlife—when it occurs—is brief.

Contemporary culture has created new customs for the young that could not be more different. Participants don't dine, they graze. Their clothes are informal. They mix up public activities with private pleasures, extending impromptu performances into late-night conversations with actors or meeting with friends to schmooze before attending unscheduled events arranged by cell phone at the last minute.

It is in small performance spaces containing only a few hundred seats where these new, younger audiences can be found. Tickets are inexpensive and programs informal, encouraging a drop-in attitude. Increasingly, viewing a performance is not the primary event of a night out but rather an anchor for a full evening's exploration in an area offering many other activities.

It is interesting to compare the following three projects: small-capacity, nonprofit theaters with loyal—if dissimilar—audiences, all built at the same time with a mission of presenting diverse contemporary programs. The three have legitimately arrived at different architectural results within the same formal enclosure: a rectangular box. I can imagine grumbling from those who would prefer architectural exteriors to present greater drama and contemporary panache, but each is, in fact, a considered response to its physical, social, financial, and program context.

Lincoln Center Theater has a fifty-five-year history. Founded as a place for New Yorkers to view classical American theater, it has become a producing organization for musical theater, plays, and solo shows. It presents both revivals and new work and was conceived as an antidote to the commercial theater of Broadway. To accomplish this, it originated an innovative nonprofit structure. The professional authority of its productions, together with its equally influential building by Eero Saarinen, require a clear architectural response.

The existing building comprises a travertine box containing the book stacks of the New York Public Library for the Performing Arts, placed above the Vivian Beaumont Theater's 1,080 seats. Beneath that lies the 195-seat Mitzi Newhouse, used for small-scale productions. At plaza level, the public enters a glass and steel lobby overlooking a reflecting pool complete with a Henry Moore sculpture. Set atop this entire structure is the new 112-seat Claire Tow Theater.

The Fisher Theater for BAM has been specifically designed for experimentation. In the rough-and-ready spirit of BAM, it is a place of discovery, where young talent and new audiences are encouraged to explore contemporary ideas of performance brought from all over the world.

The theater is adjacent to the BAM Opera House and part of a new six-story building built behind an existing two-story structure. Restoration of this 1927 Georgian-revival landmark is not intended to replicate the past but rather to develop a vessel for exploration of the future. Entered through a street-level lobby, the theater is situated in a flexible auditorium with telescopic and loose seating for 299. Located on two levels, this seating can be used for any relationship imaginable or removed altogether, permitting audiences to stand. The theater is equipped with every possible device for light and sound projection. Above it are a rehearsal room, community facilities, support spaces, and a roof garden.

Theatre for a New Audience (TFANA) is found in a six-story volume containing 299 seats on three levels of audience seating. It is housed in a cantilevered box clad in dark, reflective metal panels. The only freestanding building of the three theaters, it is composed of a simple geometric form but achieves contrast with adjacent buildings through a cantilevered front end, lifted up to reveal the lobby's active, multilevel public space. This building will be the first permanent home for this itinerant company. Our dramatic presentation of the life within it will clearly identify a new player in the BAM Cultural District.

Sites and designs of these buildings distinguish the experience of each. The Tow Theater is reached by elevator from the Beaumont's lobby and enjoys spectacular views of the Lincoln Center plaza. BAM's Fisher Theater is set between two architecturally powerful neighbors and enjoys direct street access. TFANA's site will initially frame the theater with an open plaza to the north and south. (Future Brooklyn development will provide an unknown high-rise context, but because of the adjacent plazas, the theater's principal facade will still remain prominent.)

Although modest in size, these theaters are technically sophisticated, creating more intimate experiences than those found in houses built for large-scale spectacle. Their basic purpose does not lie in financial reward; instead, they are built to explore ideas. Each is intended to give young talent a place to perform and young audiences a place of discovery. All three buildings encourage a vigorous attitude toward exploring the audience-performer relationship and the nature of live performance itself. No two are found in the same urban context, and their architectural variations on the premise of a rectangular box display a pleasing variety.

The Claire Tow Theater
at Lincoln Center
New York, New York

The New York City Landmarks Preservation Commission has traditionally opposed the placement of a new building on top of a landmark. Lincoln Center, however, is not a landmark; if it were, its imaginative update by Diller Scofidio + Renfro would not have been possible. The last element of Lincoln Center's current building program, the Claire Tow Theater, houses LCT3, an initiative to present new plays to younger audiences as an energetic complement to the Vivian Beaumont Theater's main-stage productions of theater classics and large-scale musicals.

In the powerful architectural environment of Lincoln Center, designing this addition to the Beaumont Theater was unusually challenging. The structural directness of Eero Saarinen's building was the result of a difficult collaboration with Gordon Bunshaft of Skidmore, Owings & Merrill. Bunshaft designed the portion of the complex that would contain the New York Public Library's performing-arts collection, while Saarinen's contribution would house a totally new institutional theater. These two strong-willed architects were asked to work together to achieve a unified design that would harmonize with the Metropolitan Opera House as well as another new structure, the nearby Philharmonic Hall (intended to replace Carnegie Hall). The result is one of the best and most inventive theaters at Lincoln Center.

Our task in designing a rooftop addition to the Beaumont was to ensure that it would complement, not overshadow, its host structure. Saarinen and Bunshaft's design combined two institutions by placing the library's book stacks in a travertine box suspended over the Beaumont's lobby and around its stage house. Rather than oppose these simple forms with a new geometry, our new theater's two-story volume is set back against the stage tower and supported by three 165-foot steel trusses, which are held up in turn by the theater's four-by-four-foot square concrete columns. Our three new facades are covered by a translucent screen of white aluminum tubes that shields exterior glass walls from sunlight. Not visible except at a distance, this gauzy box complements Saarinen's hard-edged, stone-clad volume and seems to recede against its solid form.

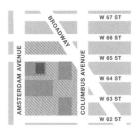

Bernard Gersten
Executive producer of
Lincoln Center Theater

BG: I love the Vivian Beaumont Theater. I think it's wonderful as a building and one of the great theaters in North America.

Young writers shouldn't write for a specific theater. They should write their plays, and we'll figure out how to do them. Although there's this idea that there are certain plays that are well suited for a thrust stage, and there are certain plays made for proscenium theaters, I don't believe that's true at all. I think that the idea of a theater originates with primitive human beings who said, "Look we have this nice fire. Why don't we sit around this fire and tell each other stories." That was the first theatrical activity. And the Greeks translated that into an arena. And so the theater evolved over thousands of years. So whatever theater you end up in, embrace it and don't complain about it all the time. People complained about this theater too much.

MF: Does Lincoln Center Theater ever do Shakespeare?

BG: We've done a number of Shakespeare plays: *Comedy of Errors*, *Twelfth Night*, *As You Like It*, *King Lear*.

MF: I went to see *A Winter's Tale*.

BG: Where?

MF: At the armory.
Did you go to that?

During the day, a changing play of light and shade on the exterior screen allows glimpses of the new front truss, reinforcing Saarinen's original structural scheme. At night, interior illumination clarifies how this truss supports all activities on the two floors within.

The public's arrival sequence begins in the Beaumont lobby, continues by elevator through the library's stack space, and concludes on the roof. At the end of a glass arrival hallway with views to the north and east, the upper lobby opens out to a rooftop terrace that offers startling vistas of the Lincoln Center plaza and the city beyond. Materials and finishes are low-key and simple. A sculpture by Kiki Smith provides a counterpoint of animation and sparkling illumination to this new rooftop public space.

Elevator access for audiences from the plaza level and service access from the concourse a level below are complicated by the passage through the library stacks. Because elevator machinery is unsightly and transparent glass requires expensive maintenance, shafts are enclosed in textured channel glass, giving the moving cabs, which are illuminated above and below, a ghostlike presence when viewed from outside.

The theater itself contains 112 seats set in a permanent bowl-like configuration. Seats are fixed in a frontal position to permit the simplest form of storytelling, instead of leaving audience configuration an open question for each production. There is no proscenium, although one could be made with scenery. More important, the stage is completely open so that performers and directors can choose platforms and

BG: I did. I think it did cost a fortune.

MF: I hope they made it back.

BG: Why would they make it back? It's not-for-profit.

MF: Or at least broke even.

BG: No, no. Not-for-profit, you spend money. The whole world isn't about making money. People think they lose money. I don't think money is lost. Money is spent, not lost. Money goes to actors and stagehands and people who fabricate theater. That's not lost money—that's spent money. That's what makes the world go round. Lost money is every time a bomb explodes or a bullet is shot. That's lost money. At best it kills somebody. And what's so good about that? We don't lose money. We spend money. We get the money that we get, and we spend it. We're spenders.

MF: That's good. Very good.

BG: Yeah. Well, capitalism has been the ruin of the middle class.

André Bishop
Artistic director of Lincoln Center Theater

AB: The theater is a profession that needs the energy that young people have. The nonprofit theater is why we are, in my opinion, living in a golden age of American playwriting, and we just don't know it. Not just in New York—there are hundreds and hundreds and hundreds of theaters all over the country, in big cities and smaller towns.

I spent many, many early years in the service of new American writing. I was completely unsuited for the job I was hired to do at Lincoln Center. It took me a number of years to really figure out what the job was. The Beaumont— even though it's been a hugely successful theater for us—was, of course, years ago considered hopeless. The program of the Beaumont—the directors and designers and, to some degree, the plays—was the thing I knew

elevations that permit actors to communicate directly with their audiences in any presentation format.

To attract young audiences, LCT3 will make tickets available at lower prices, with a generally relaxed staff offering refreshments intended to encourage mingling and easy conversation before and after performances and during intermissions. The theater's public spaces are therefore designed to be informal, and its unique rooftop views of the plaza and surrounding buildings offer an added attraction.

Our straightforward organization of the plan and its deference to the Saarinen building must be seen as a deliberate response to his exceptional design. The two structures are both physically and symbolically tied together. Although our addition certainly is prominent, it does not upstage Saarinen's work, aiming instead to complement his basic forms and organization and to represent a continuity of expression.

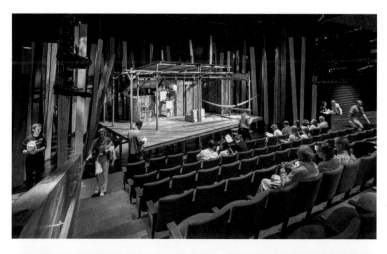

<u>Top</u> Auditorium
<u>Bottom</u> Rehearsal room

absolutely nothing about when I got here. And, curiously, I always say this to myself: I feel it's the one thing I've really done well—the programming of the Beaumont.

I had this idea that we start a third theater. And it took many, many years of persuading people that we needed to develop our own artists here. My only interest in this was to feed Lincoln Center Theater, so that people who work in LCT3 would eventually start working in the Mitzi or the Beaumont. We finally got this going. The board approved, and we started doing the work before we built the building.

We've started working with a lot of gifted artists who are having their work done in many other places. I said, "Where do you think we should have this? Should we come downtown?" And, fortunately, everyone said, "You've got to do it at Lincoln Center. Because we as younger artists don't want to be your little annex on West Eighteenth Street—we want to be with the big boys. We want to be alongside your other theaters, and to be accepted as part of the LCT family."

<u>MF</u>: Had you planned to put it on the roof?

<u>AB</u>: No, we didn't. We had planned to put it anywhere but the roof, because we didn't know how we'd get up to the roof: the library was up there. And it has been a formidable task to build this theater on the roof.

But it's small and modest. The whole point was to produce as many productions as we could, and have them fully designed, but modestly, with limited runs, and at twenty dollars a ticket. It's been, in a way, a folly.

<u>MF</u>: Did people object to putting the building on top of the Saarinen?

<u>AB</u>: Yes. There was quite a lot of to-do, and what helped us was the modesty of it and also that the goals for the theater were unimpeachable. You couldn't fight it. And Hugh's presence was helpful.

Richard B. Fisher Building
Brooklyn Academy of Music
Brooklyn, New York

The new Fisher Building at the Brooklyn Academy of Music is mandated by landmark law to be architecturally compatible with its two unusual large-scale neighbors as well as the existing structure upon which it is built: a two-story, Georgian-revival former home to the Salvation Army. The seventy-foot-tall BAM Opera House, built in 1908, is immediately to the north, and the thirty-four-story, preposterously phallic Williamsburgh Savings Bank of 1929 (now a residential condominium) is to the south. Our new theater forms a hybrid of the 1929 brick Salvation Army building and a new six-story building set behind. The new volume contains a 250-seat flexible theater together with rehearsal, community, and administrative spaces, all topped by a roof garden. The addition, although set back by twenty-four feet from the original street facade, needed to be carefully designed to complement adjacent and dissimilar landmark buildings.

Although every effort was made to design a contemporary and highly flexible performing space for the Fisher Theater, the Landmarks Commission insisted our new facade defer to the past through the use of masonry and a simple, symmetrical fenestration pattern that would complement the neighboring street wall. The focus of our composition was therefore knitting together the walls of three disparate landmark structures to form a harmonious grouping. Combining these into a coherent whole took precedent over developing an adventurous reflection of BAM's Next Wave programming.

A composite facade was established with the insertion of a central two-story glass window played off against smaller windows above. The result is a symmetrical background building whose textured brick consciously refers to its neighbor's decorative masonry walls. Would BAM have been better served by a vigorous new design that would forcefully announce itself as an original idea? Could this new facade assert itself with the same authority as the BAM canopy? Was the Landmarks Commission wrong to insist upon such a background solution? Alas, nothing in the architecture of the existing three buildings offers a sufficiently strong design premise to have held its own against an aggressive new

Joe Melillo
Executive producer and artistic director of the Brooklyn Academy of Music

JM: I think young, emerging artists need to be encouraged to do experiments in their work. We're a city of alternative theater spaces, where a lot of experimentation happens, and that's where I hope that the critics would be generous to the alternative spaces.

At the Fisher Building, because the space is flexible, I have commissioned a group of Brooklyn artists to do new work exploring different spatial relationships.

All the seats move and they disappear. No seats—that's my favorite configuration. I'm looking forward to one upcoming production—a visual arts installation that will be animated by visual artists using performative techniques to engage the audience. So the audience is standing and interacting with what they are creating.

Another upcoming performance using open space will be staged by a cinematic multimedia artist. Audience members will walk in one by one to begin the experience. So it's a different kind of interaction. It will be interactive; it will be participatory. It is very much about how performance and visual art work in a spatial environment. So one week that will be the experience, and the next week you'll have 250 seats set up for a very formal dance presentation. Dancers—scenic design. Although our studies show a wide range of possibilities (some of which can be found below), none avoid the conceit of boldness for its own sake; for that reason, any of them probably would have appeared dated and naïve a few years later. Instead, this quiet addition to the streetscape permits the existing structures to be seen on their own terms, each making a clear statement about the time it was built.

Replacing this landmark building's original wood-paneled doors with sheets of glass to reveal the two-story lobby's activities to the street will animate the center of this block. By illuminating the lobby and hanging cutout banners at right angles to the facade, BAM identifies the structure without the expense of a marquee. Visible from several angles,

environment—sound—250. So each week it's going to have a different configuration. It's like a playground for adults.

Karen Brooks Hopkins
President of the Brooklyn
Academy of Music

MF: Could you give us your ideas about how you are different at BAM from, say, Carnegie Hall and Lincoln Center?

KBH: Well, first of all we are in Brooklyn, and that already sets us geographically apart.

Facade studies for Richard B. Fisher Building, 2011

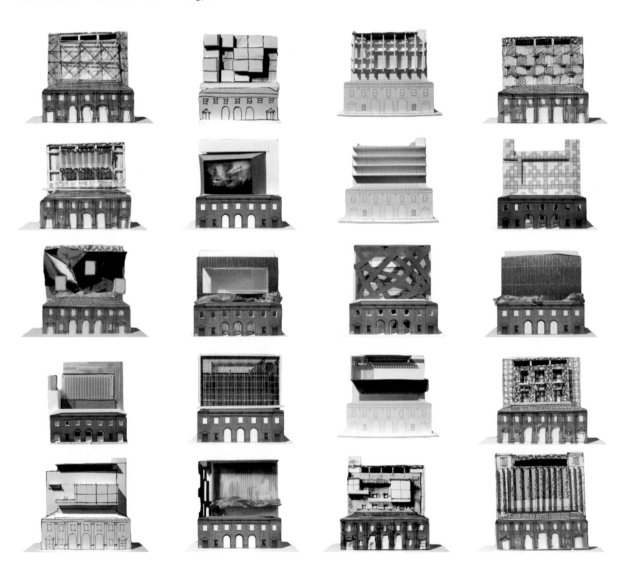

the animated, illuminated interiors of both the original structure and the new addition will clearly announce performances are at hand.

Well-marked auditorium entrances at street level and a staircase with illuminated risers make patterns of circulation obvious between the street-level floor of theater entry and a lower lobby where restrooms and refreshments are found. As is often the case in New York's older theater buildings, intimacy just short of congestion gives the public areas their character, despite a mirrored upper wall that helps visually expand the limited space.

After experiencing the lobby, visitors are surprised to discover the four-story volume that defines the performance space: an enclosure of dark-blue acoustically reflective and absorbent surfaces. Several unconventional elements combine to make this long-sought small-scale space more intimate and flexible: a transparent wire grid stretches below stage lighting equipment instead of catwalks, and telescoping movable seating permits a variety of configurations. As artistic director Joe Melillo notes, young performers prefer a mix of media as well as less-formal seating arrangements that can sometimes change even in the course of a single production. Video is often used together with unexpected sources of sound. This new theater is designed to accommodate a lively range of changing relationships and activities and to reach out to young audiences through adventuresome programming, continuing BAM's tradition of great variety and modest ticket prices.

Entrance lobby

Second, we are a historic institution. The original BAM was built on Montague Street and opened in 1861, burned to the ground in 1903, and was rebuilt here in 1908 with the architects Herts & Tallant. And the conception of this building was that it would have multiple spaces for performance and rehearsal and so on, so I don't think that there was anything else quite like it at the time. BAM is really not a landlord. BAM is a presenter, and we curate all the programs that happen in our facilities.

MF: Are you doing this in Europe and in Asia?

KBH: We're interested in global BAM; we're interested in local BAM at the Fisher Building; we're interested in the Cultural District becoming the great urban cultural district for the twenty-first century; and we think that there is a real opportunity, now that more institutions are building here, for the district to be completed and really thrive.

MF: Are there obstacles in working with landmark buildings, like the Fisher for instance?

KBH: Yes. There are financial obstacles; there are space restrictions; there are a lot of rules about design and what you can do and zoning and all kinds of things. There are many, many obstacles.

MF: What do you do to overcome those obstacles?

KBH: You work through each, one at a time.

The Merchant of Venice
MAR. 3
THROUGH
MAY 15
CYMBELINE
JULY.2
THROUGH
SEPT. 10
THEATRE
FOR A NEW
AUDIENCE
MACBETH
SEPT. 25
THROUGH
NOV. 15
Notes from Underground
SEPT. 25
THROUGH
NOV. 15
THE JOHN DOE BUILDING
SEX
GREED
FOLLY
DEATH

Theatre for a New Audience
Brooklyn, New York

This project represents a model for how the arts can act as catalysts for urban planning. In place of the usual solutions focusing on transportation networks, housing, or commercial square footage, the scheme for Theatre for a New Audience (TFANA) demonstrates how community life can be brought into public space.

Alas, construction in the BAM Cultural District (with the exception of the Mark Morris Dance Center and the Harvey Theater) has concentrated so far on conventional development of high-rise condominiums, which don't include living or working spaces for artists or public space. To counteract this oversight, New York City is building a new home for Theatre for a New Audience, a sprightly off-Broadway company that has been in existence for thirty-three years without a permanent facility. The theater will have flexible seating for 299 in a five-story box built to accommodate a variety of audience-performer relationships. Surrounded on the east and west by a public plaza designed by Ken Smith, this small building will at first appear as an almost freestanding structure facing Ashland Place, diagonally opposite the BAM Opera House.

Imagine a theater company without a permanent company of actors or its own home. Imagine how artistic director Jeffrey Horowitz could consistently elicit fine performances to animate his constantly changing venues. Imagine audiences sufficiently loyal to follow the company all over the city, whether in Manhattan or Brooklyn, uptown or downtown; clearly the work must be of notably high quality to bring audiences together, and indeed, the achievements of TFANA over the years have identified it as a special resource. (All this came about by accident; the company was founded with money from Horowitz's settlement with an insurance company, which paid him significant damages after a floor of blazing polyurethane scorched his feet as he escaped from his apartment during a renovation.)

Brooklyn is a city of masonry—predominately brick with stone embellishment, built before the current craze for glass walls. Theater space must be enclosed, separate from the outside world, and

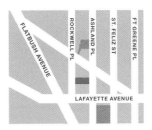

Jeffrey Horowitz
Founding artistic director of
Theatre for a New Audience

JH: I said, "I want a theater inspired by the Cottesloe Theatre at the Royal National Theatre in London. That's what this is— this is not up for discussion. It has a certain aesthetic. It's a totally flexible space."

Then I said, "I want to get a theater consultant. I want to get the guys who built the Cottesloe, because proportion is everything about that space. And I love Peter Brook's work. I want to get the technical director of the designer who worked with Peter Brook." Peter Brook was all over the world, and he would send a person ahead to go into a city and find a space and ensure the proportions would work. This guy's name is Jean-Guy Lecat.

I said to Hugh, "I want you to come visit theaters with me." And we went to Philadelphia; we went to the McCarter in Princeton, New Jersey, where Hugh had designed a 299-seat theater, the Berlind. We went to Paris, we went to London. We went to Liverpool. We went outside of London. And we went to the Cottesloe, of course. We could see in all these theaters that if you got the proportion wrong, it was dead. It felt like a flat fish. There was no exchange with the audience. Hugh took the trouble to do all of that. He was genuinely creatively engaged with this.

We would have discussions— very long discussions—about black. Is black a good color? Because you've heard of a black box. Well,

therefore, TFANA's walls are blank except for the great glass lobby facade facing Ashland Place. Our basic box is a hard-edged simple enclosure clad with reflective metal panels to deliberately set this small structure off from its present and future neighbors. The simple gesture of lifting the cladding up at the front corners encourages entry from the east or west, and permits an unobstructed view of the public space within through the transparent principal facade. The interior is visible through a five-story glass wall with light steel mullions that is suspended from above and cantilevered from below. These two structural systems join in a horizontal beam from which light illuminates the plaza below.

The Royal National Theatre in London provides a precedent for the interior design of TFANA's new theater. Its small Cottesloe Theatre, designed by Iain Mackintosh of Theatre Projects Consultants, has been home to a variety of successful productions since its 1977 construction in found space behind the National Theatre's two larger main stages. Jeffrey Horowitz wanted to bring the Cottesloe's special construct to New York. Following this model, TFANA's performing area can be configured in many different ways or even made into a small, independent theater when the full volume is not in use. It can also be joined with a rehearsal hall behind the rear wall to create a performance space one hundred feet long. Proscenium, thrust, runway, or theater-in-the-round productions are all possible, from intimately focused productions to wide-open spectacle.

it can't be a black box. It can be a dark-gray box, a dark-blue box. And we'd have endless discussions about black—there's actually a green-black, a blue-black, a red-black. I learned a lot about black.

And then I remember a very important discussion we had. I said the Cottesloe Theatre is about change—it keeps changing. And there's no one way to do a Shakespeare play, a classical play. We kept coming back to certain principles, which were simplicity and ability to express change. I think probably the most overused word in theater is "innovative." And we went through lots of debates, and he listened very carefully.

Then the next thing that happened was that the location of the site was changed by the city twice. So we call Hugh and we say, "Hugh, the building is going to have to shrink by seventy-five hundred square feet and we're going to have to cut I don't know how many millions, and we have nineteen days." I said, "Just take a deep breath. We're going to have to do it. Otherwise, the building really is finished." Hugh has vision, but he's not rigid. And that enabled us to continue. You can't imagine the stress.

MF: Will you only do Shakespeare?

JH: First of all, we don't only do Shakespeare. We do Shakespeare along with a lot of other great writing, because Shakespeare is not in a vacuum. It's part of a continuum. When you do Shakespeare, it should be as if it's a new play, as if you're uncovering a connection between that writing and who you are. That's what makes it classic—because people keep uncovering the connections for their time. So the thing about the Cottesloe Theatre and about this space is that you can do all kinds of different writing. You can do new plays, Shakespeare; you can do them in multiple configurations. And it's not expensive to reconfigure.

The theater has this concept of transparency between the public space and the park. Landscape architect Ken Smith was hired by the city, but it was Hugh's idea that we should have mullion-free

A visitor's sequence of arrival begins on the street, where the facade is embellished by a giant display of changeable banners designed by Milton Glaser. These banners, along with illuminated signage and varied projections, will take the place of a conventional marquee. The entry sequence continues through the multilevel lobby to the subdued four-story volume of the auditorium, which is set one level up from the street. Movement between the auditorium and two upper seating levels is visible through the glass facade and animates the building during performance hours. Because seating is flexible and entered at different levels and vantage points depending upon the production, many different relationships between audience and performer can be created.

Having performed in so many different theaters around the city, TFANA can at last continue its explorations securely located in its own home.

Theatre for a New Audience under construction

glass so that the park flows into the theater and the theater flows into the lobby. And the entrance shouldn't be in the front—it should be on the sides, so that as people are coming from the BAM Opera House and the Harvey, they're coming into a space that's flowing out into this park instead of having a door that blocks the visual flow. The park wraps around, and you enter from either side. You have a building that's symmetrical and also emphasizes the symmetry, so that was wonderful.

We were interested in having a connection with the neighborhood. In all three sites proposed by the city there was a sense of a connection with the neighborhood. The first site was actually oriented as if you were facing Flatbush. So the idea of people looking in was always attractive to us. I had been working with the artist Milton Glaser, and we got the idea that we could create a fly system, and Milton could design fabrics that would have titles, so this becomes the marquee. In the windows there are plasma screens, and in the park there are stanchions for the advertising, but we decided to eliminate the traditional idea of a marquee, and have Milton's work essentially be the marquee.

Something that Hugh saw from very early on is that to have a building of this design in this location in downtown Brooklyn, the fourth largest city in America—it really is a renaissance of Brooklyn. It is the next major arts center in New York.

MF: Has Harvey Lichtenstein seen this?

JH: Absolutely. Harvey was the head of what was then called the BAM Local Development Corporation. Then that morphed into Downtown Brooklyn Partnership. But the BAM Cultural District was a dream of Harvey's when he was at BAM.

The theater was unveiled by the Mayor in 2005 and it didn't break ground until 2011. That's a long time trying to explain to the press that this is not a bad story but an ongoing story.

THEATRE FOR A NEW AUDIENCE

Afterword

We not only get the politicians we deserve, we get the architects we deserve. Their achievements are as much a public as a professional concern because society's most elemental aspirations find expression in new construction.

Now that we are at the end of this investigation into making architecture, my debt to the nature of theater and the importance of context—both physical and social—is clear. The essential nature of architecture lies in embracing awareness of our physical, financial, and historical environment. Knowledge of theater can help inform creation of buildings— not through imitating the illusions of painted scenery but through understanding how buildings are discovered and experienced by the public.

Theater publicly reveals the human condition through appealing to both intellect and emotion. Architecture, whether lowly or exalted, can do the same. Earlier generations borrowed many of theater's techniques and technologies, creating spatial realms with scenery that would not be realizable through permanent construction. Contemporary juxtapositions of scale, exaggerated manipulations of decorative pattern, or the use of theatrical lighting to establish character in contemporary public spaces continue to suggest that architects are again being influenced by the stage.

Tomorrow continues to remain unknown, except for the certainty that technology is changing society faster than anyone fully understands. With electronic exchanges that instantly create networks joining words and images (all in color), or 3D models materializing out of thin air, the nineteenth-century hierarchy of organizational structures is fast fading away. Commonly accepted and skillful management forms that once sustained global industrial, political, social, and economic systems in the industrial age are now being challenged by less-hierarchical communities connected by cell phones. Strangers all over the world can communicate with a random organizational structure that replaces how collective decisions were once made.

The built environment of cities offers insight into society's priorities. In the nineteenth century, Frederick Law Olmsted's parks were developed from a belief that access to nature was essential for the health and welfare of all citizens. Their construction is one of New York's great accomplishments.

A similar public awareness of the importance of the natural environment is with us again. Even though New York's unparalleled wealth has been based upon an industrial approach to manufacturing, food supply, transportation, and management, that premise is now being questioned. It is becoming obvious that if in the twenty-first century we continue our current practices of ill-considered consumerism, our collective future will be threatened. The public's new awareness of environmental issues now challenges architects to accept responsibility for more efficient use of materials. Construction and maintenance of buildings use 60 percent of all the energy consumed in the United States. Since we build with finite natural resources, we must find more efficient ways to use them and explore new or renewable forms of energy.

New buildings in cities, whatever the scale, become part of the larger urban context. Over time they create a panoply of changing relationships as new and old respond to each other. For this exchange to work successfully, each new project must be authentic, clearly stating its purpose and composition. Even brutal juxtapositions are preferable to chicanery, so long as the end results speak clearly. Curiosity about a building's historical legacy—whatever its stylistic premise—and the insights gained from the human experience it embodies all become part of our common architectural heritage.

Contrasted with the spirited investigations of contemporary architects, modernism's call for formal order can perhaps now be better understood in historical context. Many new ways to conceive, construct, and live in buildings are at hand. We therefore can no longer plausibly engage in specific predictions or even successfully cite a manifesto.

Nonetheless, this book represents the long-term goal of making places that support curiosity and encourage community activity. Such shared human concerns—whatever their physical expression—are obviously as important as the mechanics of architectural design. In a changing world, they continue to define the best of our future as well as ways to enhance understanding of the past.

My profession should remember that the way to show architectural mastery is not to embellish the importance of the architect, but to enhance the experience of the visitor. After all, the public, not architectural theory, is our ultimate judge.

Acknowledgments

Collaboration has guided the spirit of this publication from the beginning, starting with those who sponsored, designed, and built the projects recorded here.

The American Academy in Rome awarded me the title of Resident during April, May, and June of 2011. There, surrounded by its calm beauty and supported by Adele Chatfield-Taylor's inspired presidency and Christopher Celenza's oversight, I was able to hink through the organization and initial writing of this book. This respite from everyday demands, together with the great cultural legacy of Rome, made it possible to discover what I wanted to say about my life in architecture, and I am most grateful for this unexpected honor. It gave me a rare opportunity.

Mildred Friedman is appropriately acknowledged on the title page, but I want to express here my appreciation for her original suggestion to include clients' voices in this project. Her participation in drawing clients into informative discussions has made a great contribution.

The architectural photographers whose excellent work documents all twenty projects have been most generous by permitting us to use their work. Without their skill this book could not exist.

Kevin Lippert, publisher of Princeton Architectural Press, was the original supporter of this publication, providing me with the encouragement needed to write the text during my stay in Rome, then revise it in New York. His faith in the outcome has made all this possible.

My two editors, Jennifer Lippert and Sara Stemen, have shepherded and challenged me through the process of putting the whole effort together. Jennifer has consistently asked for clarity and inclusion of the human interest offered by storytelling. Sara has seamlessly worked with all of us in the name of logic and accuracy, determined to have us use language well.

Christy Banister, with the further work of James Willeford, performed invaluable early research, coordinated the endless pursuit of text and photo credits, and provided the general organization that this publication required to be both a verbally accurate and visually compelling exploration of architecture.

Abby Carlen has put together the finishing touches on this publication, with a final review that has provided great clarification of its organization and purpose. It represents an exemplary contribution.

This book's design, by Penelope Hardy, delights me from beginning to end, perfectly capturing the spirit of this enterprise. Her insightful work proves the validity and power of good graphic design.

Hugh Hardy, FAIA

Photo Credits H3 Hardy Collaboration Architecture: 54A, 134A, 139A, 202A, 202B, 202c, 212, 216, 218, 220–221; HHPA Archives: 6L, 19A, 26L, 26R, 72–73, 123R, 124L, 122R, 126B, 144L, 144A, 144B, 145L; Hugh Hardy & Associates: 28; Hugh Hardy: 6R, 219; Alex C. MacLean: 147; Balmori Associates: 195C; BAM Hamm Archives: 106A, 106B, 116L, 116R; C.K. Bill / Central Synagogue Archives: 176A; Carol M. Highsmith's America, Library of Congress, Prints and Photographs Division: 14c; Central Synagogue Archives: 176B, 176c; Cervin Robinson: 22, 24, 166A, 168, 171, 172–173; Chris Cooper: 32c, 52, 54B, 55A, 55B, 57, 58–59, 134c, 152, 155L, 155R, 156, 157A, 157B, 158, 159, 160–161, 162–163, 182B, 190, 192A, 192B, 195A, 195B, 196, 197, 198–199; Christopher Lovi: 145L, 146B, 150–151; Christy Banister: 13A; Church of St. Luke in the Fields Archives: 170; Durston Saylor: 114, 117; Eduard Hueber / Archphoto: 136, 139B, 140–141; Elena Olivo: 116A; Elliott Kaufman Photography: 19B, 62A, 64, 67, 68A, 68B, 69, 70–71, 86, 88, 89, 90A, 182A, 184, 186; Estate of Jo Mielziner: 19c; Francis Dzikowski / ESTO: 64A, 65B, 90B, 91, 92–93, 94, 96, 98, 99, 204, 206, 207A, 207B, 208–209, 210, 213, 214–215; James Cavanaugh: 44R, 97A, 97B; Jason Mrachina: 14d; Karli Cadel: 188–189; Kevin Chu / KCJP: 148–149; Kevin Roche Archives: 14A; Library of Congress, Prints and Photographs Division, HABS No. NY 32-NIAF, 5-5: 44L; Library of Congress, Prints and Photographs Division, HABS No. NY-6076-1: 13c; Mahaiwe Archives: 17L; Mark LaRosa: 17R; Michael Moran / Otto Archive, LLC: 14B, 32B, 42, 46–47, 48, 49, 50–51; Michael Simon: 10; Mick Hales: 36A; The Museum of Modern Art / Licensed by Scala / Art Resource, NY: 153B; Museum of the City of New York: 66L, 66R; Norman McGrath: 16L, 29; Patrick Lee: 9; Paul Warchol: 142; Peter Aaron / ESTO / Otto Archive, LLC: 112A, 118–119, 166B, 174, 177, 178, 179; Peter Mauss / ESTO: 102, 104, 107A, 107B, 108–109; Robert Benson: 32A, 34, 37A, 37B, 38–39, 40–41; Sara Cedar Miller: 36B; Whitney Cox: 16R, 62B, 74, 76R, 77A, 77B, 78–79, 80–81, 112B, 120, 122, 123L, 126A, 127, 128–129, 130–131; Wisconsin Center for Film and Theater Research: 76L

Published by
Princeton Architectural Press
37 East Seventh Street,
New York, New York 10003

Visit our website at www.papress.com.

Project editor   Sara E. Stemen
Design   PSNewYork.com /
                 Penny Hardy, Carren Edward Petrosyan

Special thanks to Sara Bader, Nicola Bednarek Brower, Janet Behning, Fannie Bushin, Megan Carey, Carina Cha, Andrea Chlad, Ben English, Russell Fernandez, Jan Hartman, Jan Haux, Diane Levinson, Jennifer Lippert, Jacob Moore, Katharine Myers, Margaret Rogalski, Elana Schlenker, Dan Simon, Andrew Stepanian, Paul Wagner, and Joseph Weston of Princeton Architectural Press — Kevin C. Lippert, publisher

Library of Congress Cataloging-in-Publication Data
Hardy, Hugh, 1932–
   Theater of architecture / Hugh Hardy;
   conversations with Mildred Friedman. — First edition.
   pages cm
   ISBN 978-1-61689-131-2 (hardcover : alk. paper)
1. Hardy, Hugh, 1932—Themes, motives.
2. Architecture. I. Friedman, Mildred S. II. Title.
NA737.H29A35 2013
720.92—dc23
                          2012018575